The History of
Knitting in Art

A collection of paintings, drawings, and prints
from Western art in the 19th century

by Tulasi Zimmer

The History of
Knitting in Art
A collection of paintings, drawings, and prints
from Western art in the 19th century

Cover Design by: Tulasi Zimmer

Cover painting :
"Blue Interior"
by HarrietBacker
in the 1800s

ISBN-13: 978-0-9892411-5-1
ISBN-10: 0989241157

Printed in U.S.A

CRYSTALMOON
PUBLISHING

INTRODUCTION

The process of (hand) knitting involves using two or more needles to manipulate yarn into a series of loops and knots that create a variety of fabrics and garments. The origin of knitting started from a basic need for clothing to protect the body from the elements. But today, handknitting has evolved more into a hobby and for many a source of relaxation.

It is difficult to accurately trace back when knitting was first invented, but it is believed to have originated in Egypt around 300-499. Evidence of knitting began to appear in Europe (especially in France Britain, and Germany) during the 1300s. During this time, the elastic character of the fabric became very popular and rapidly went into general use for manufacturing garments. In England, knitting was an activity or hobby that could be found in all levels of society and was not just a source of livelihood in the cottage or peasant class. Men were also believed to have been the first to knit as an occupation and knitting was generally looked upon as a refined skill.

In the Scottish Isles, knitting became a primary occupation for many people living during the 17th and 18th centuries. It was not uncommon to find whole families involved in making essential garments such as sweaters and socks and using techniques such as Fair Isle color knitting and cable stitches.

In the early 1900s knitted fabrics, previously done by hand, were now being done by machines, and handknitting gradually evolved into becoming a popular hobby.

This book is a collection of paintings, drawings, and prints, from Western art, illustrating knitting as both a hobby and an occupation during the 1800s.

Paintings

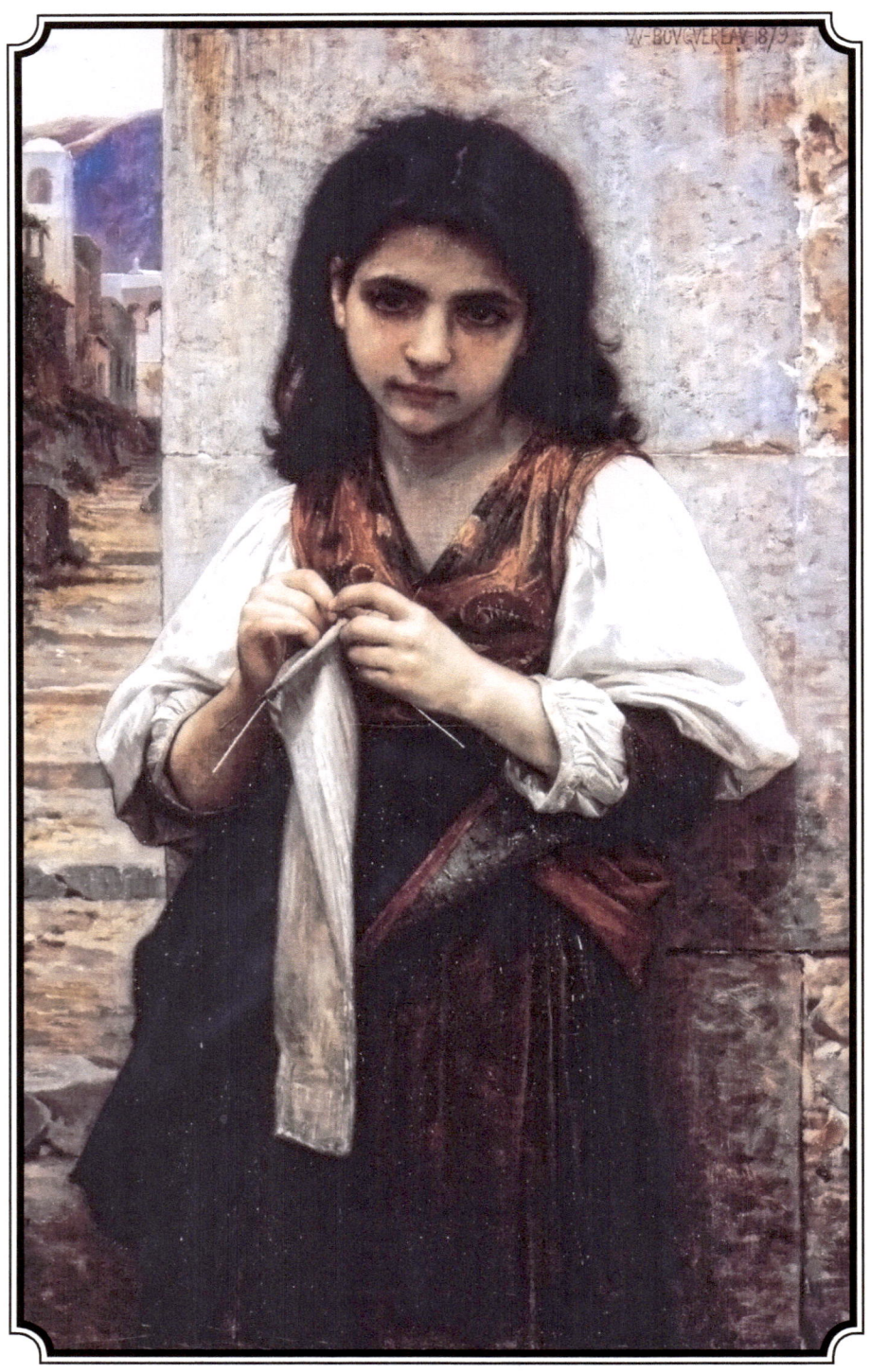

"The Tricoteuse", by William Adolphe Bouguereau
Oil, 1869

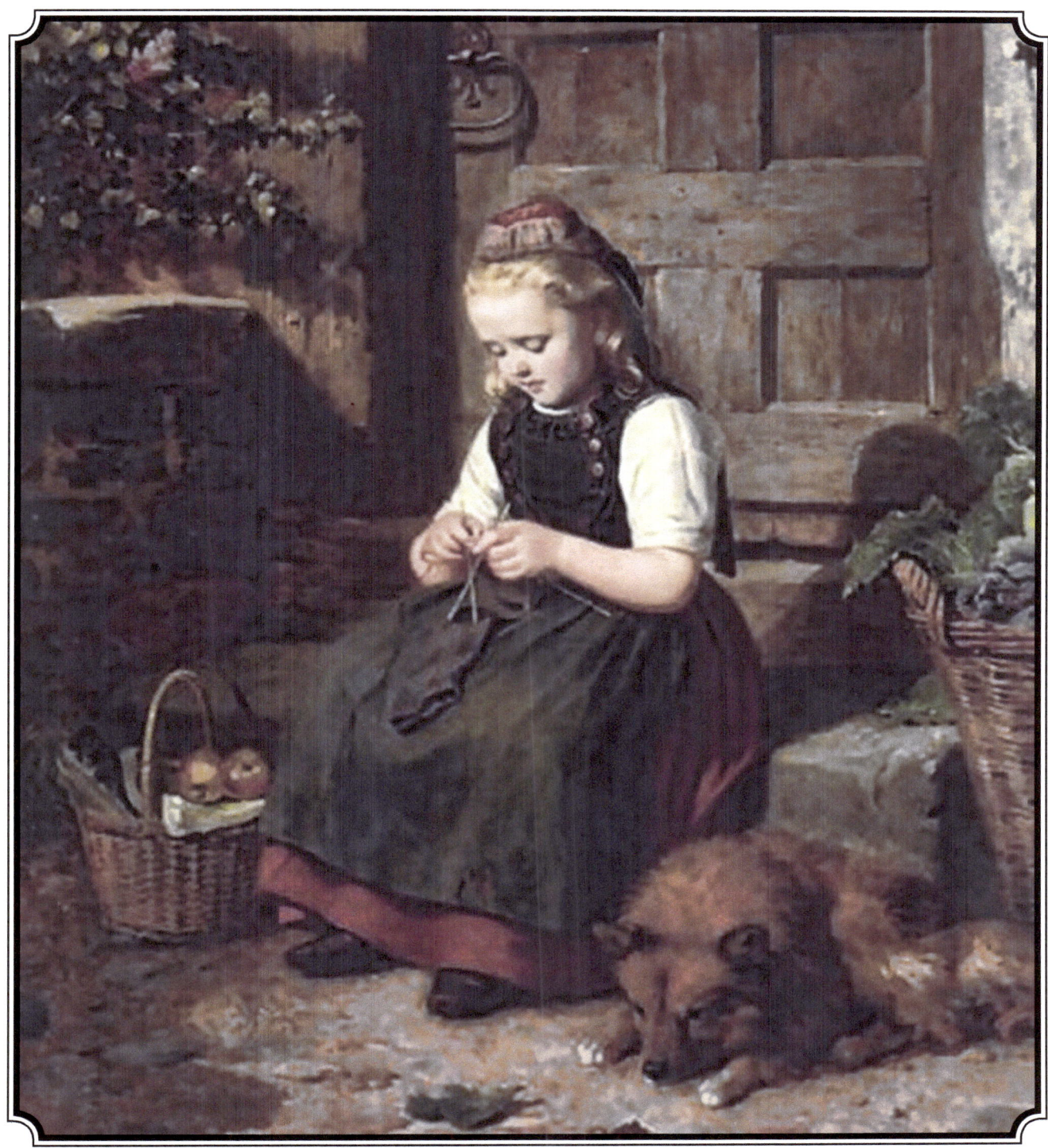

"A young girl knitting", by Auguste Dircks
Oil, 1850

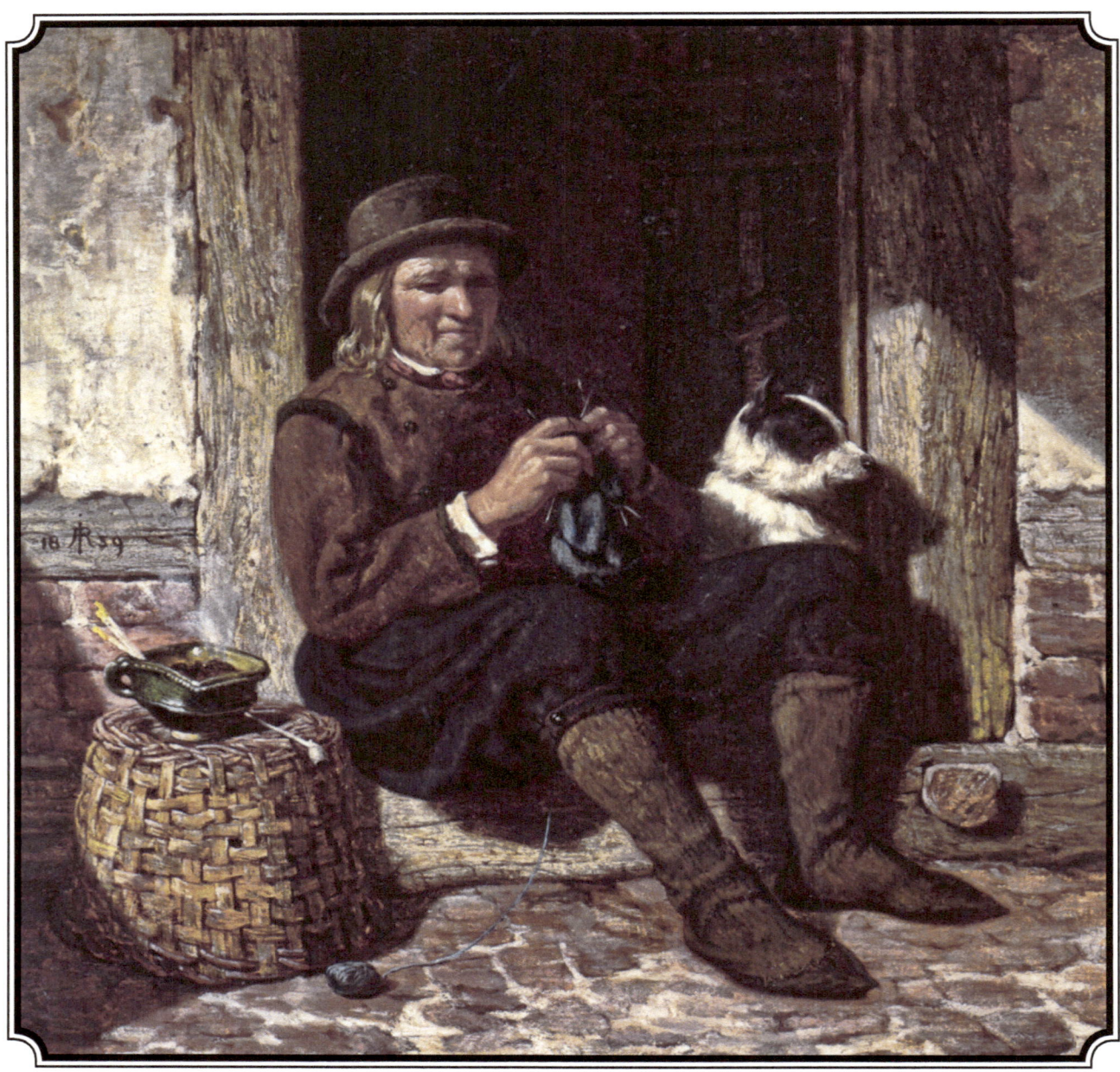

"A Man Seated in a Doorway Knitting", by Rudolf Jordan
Oil, 1837

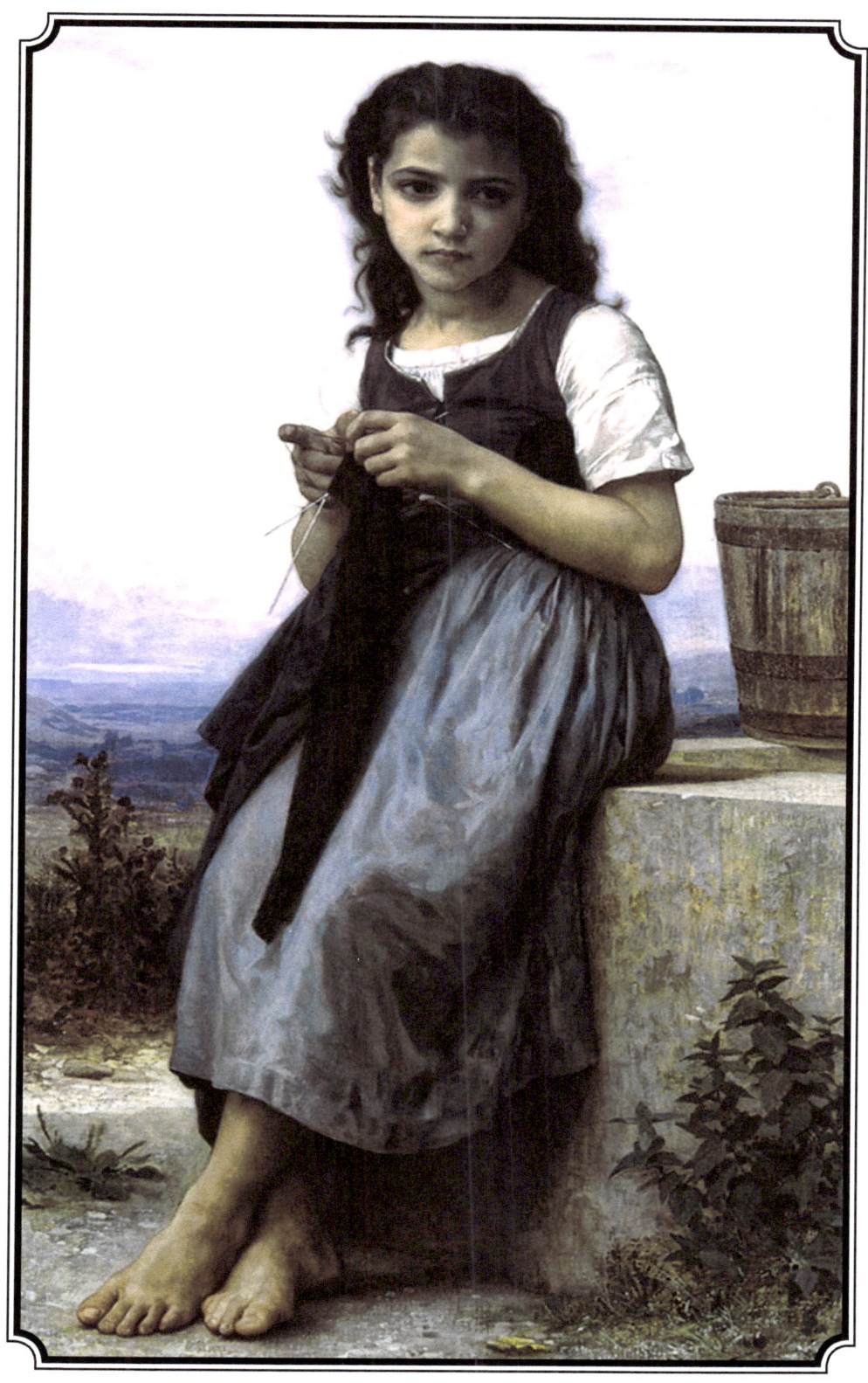

"The Knitting Girl", by William-Adolphe Bouguereau
Oil, 1869

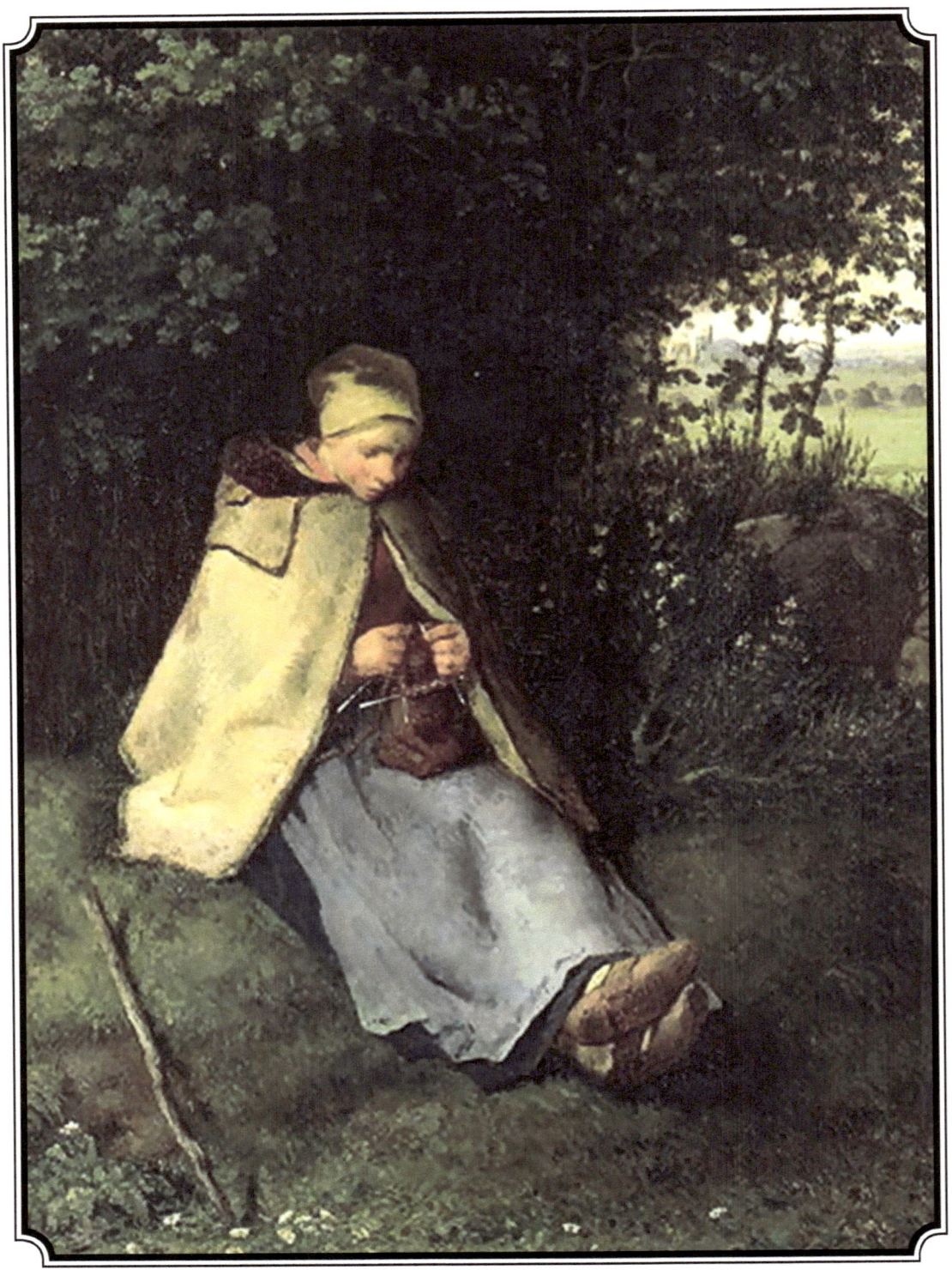

"The Knitting Sheperdess", by Jean-Francois Millet
Oil, 1856

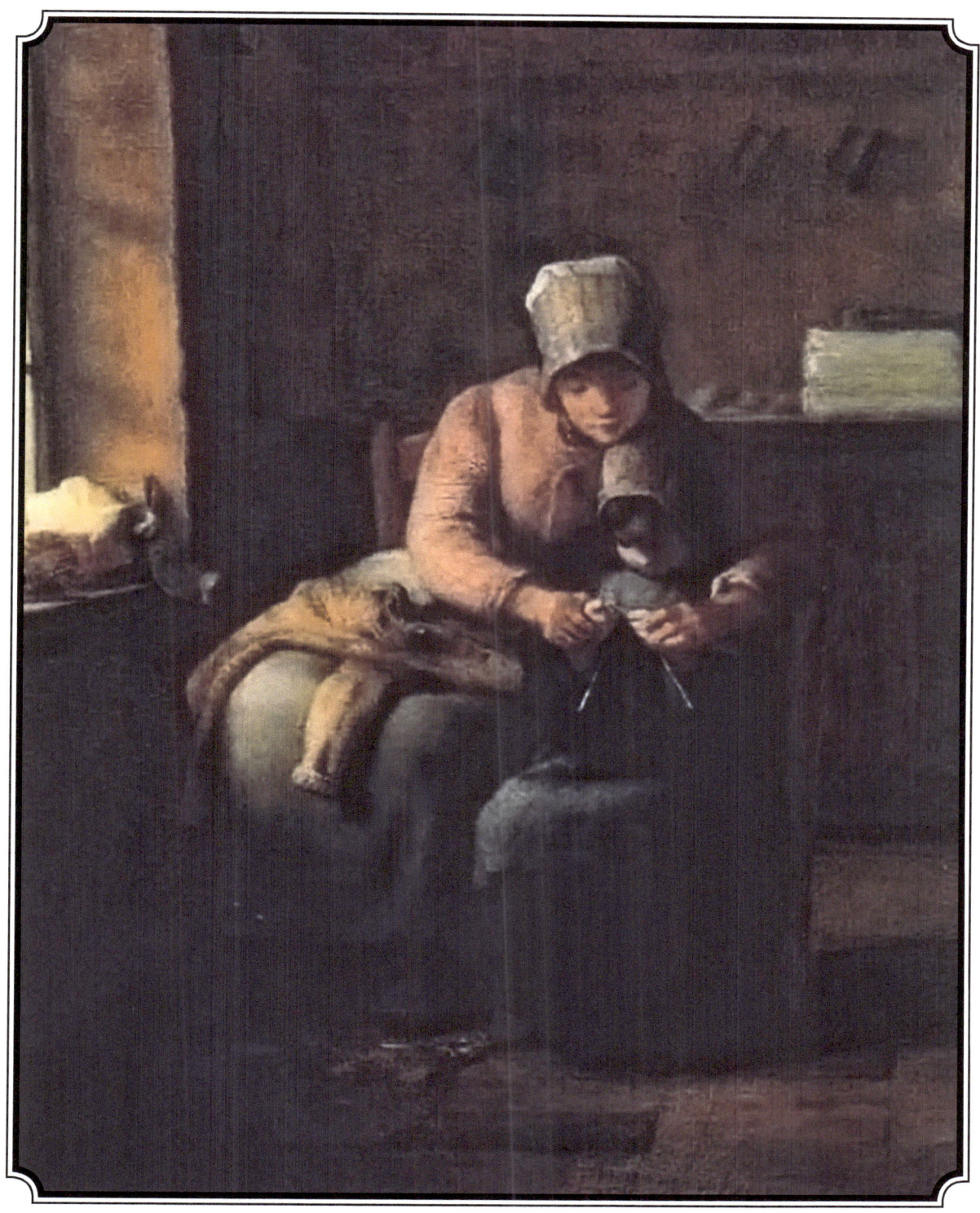

"The Knitting Lesson", by Jean-Francois Millet
Oil, 1869

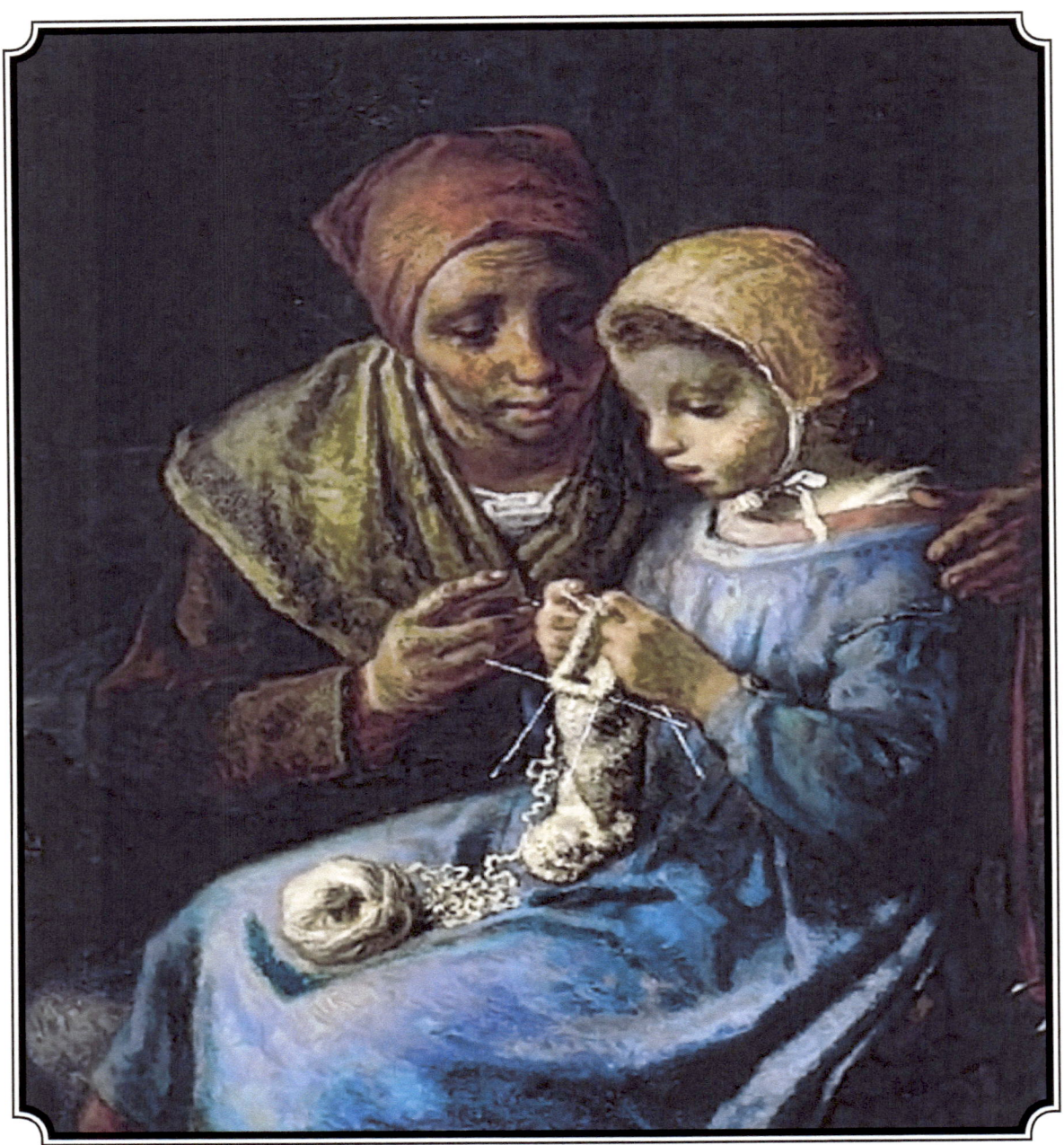

"The Knitting Lesson", by Jean-Francois Millet
Oil, 1869

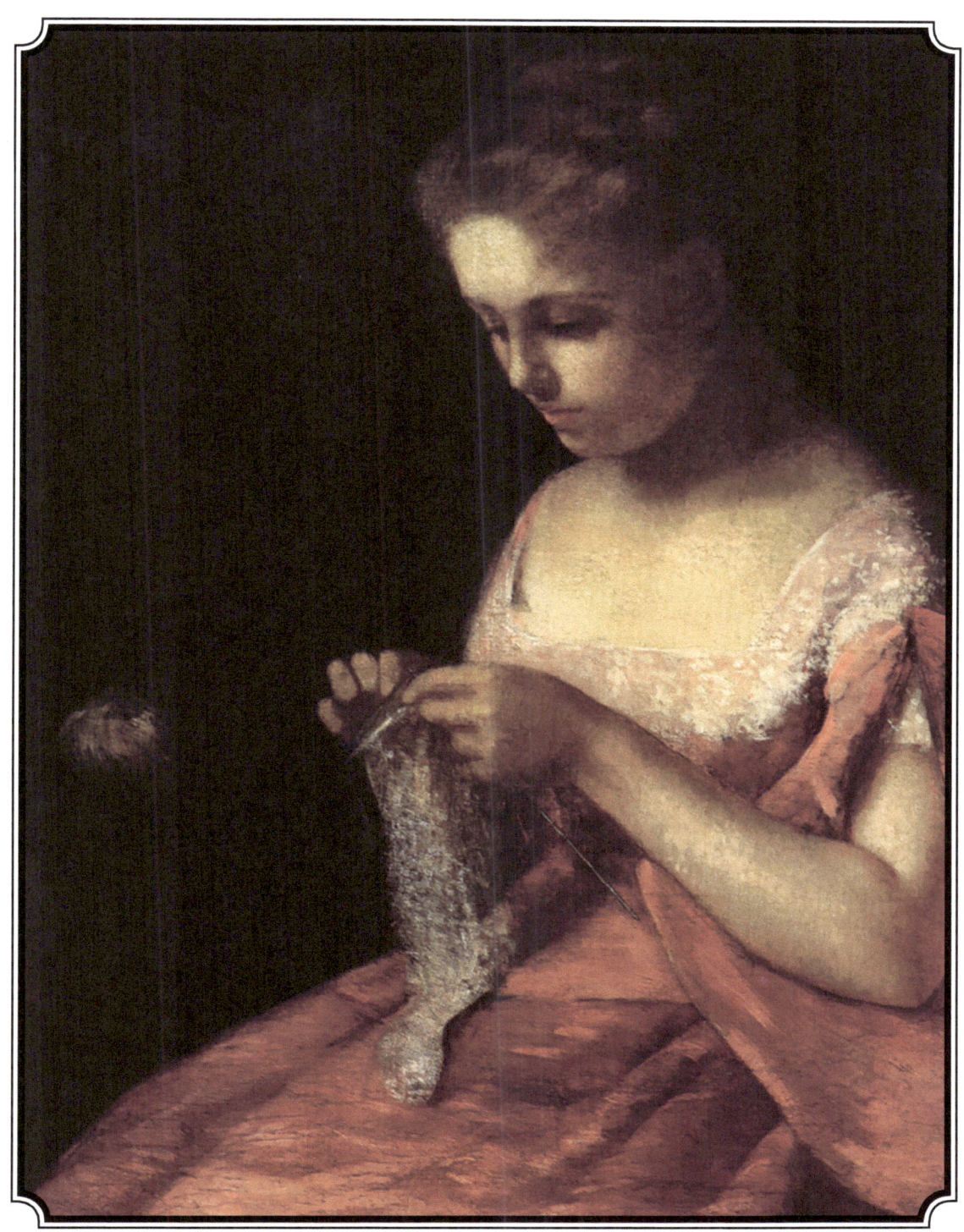

"The Young Bride:, by Mary Cassatt
Oil, 1875

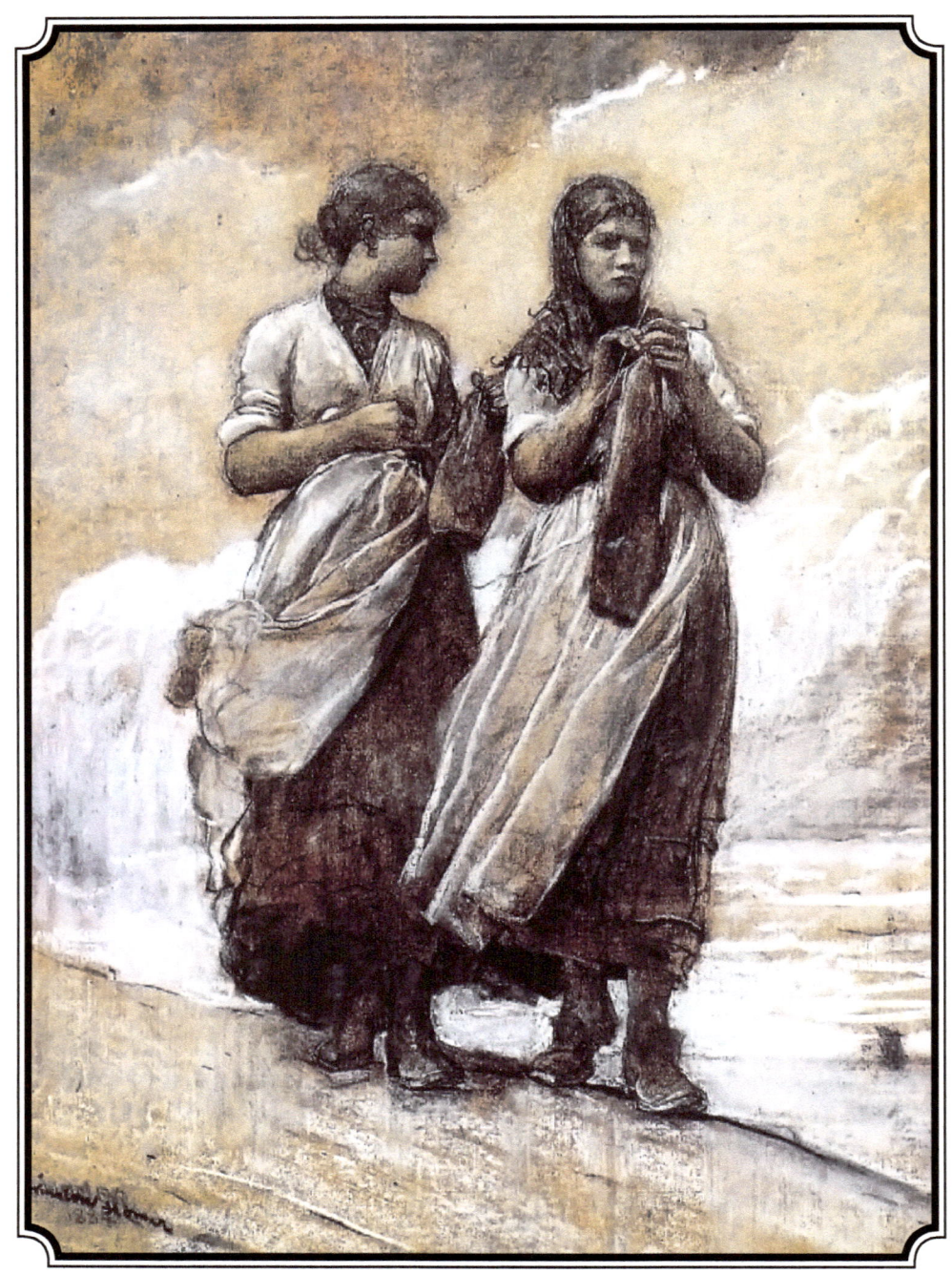

"Fishergirls on Shore" by Winslow Homer
Oil, 1884

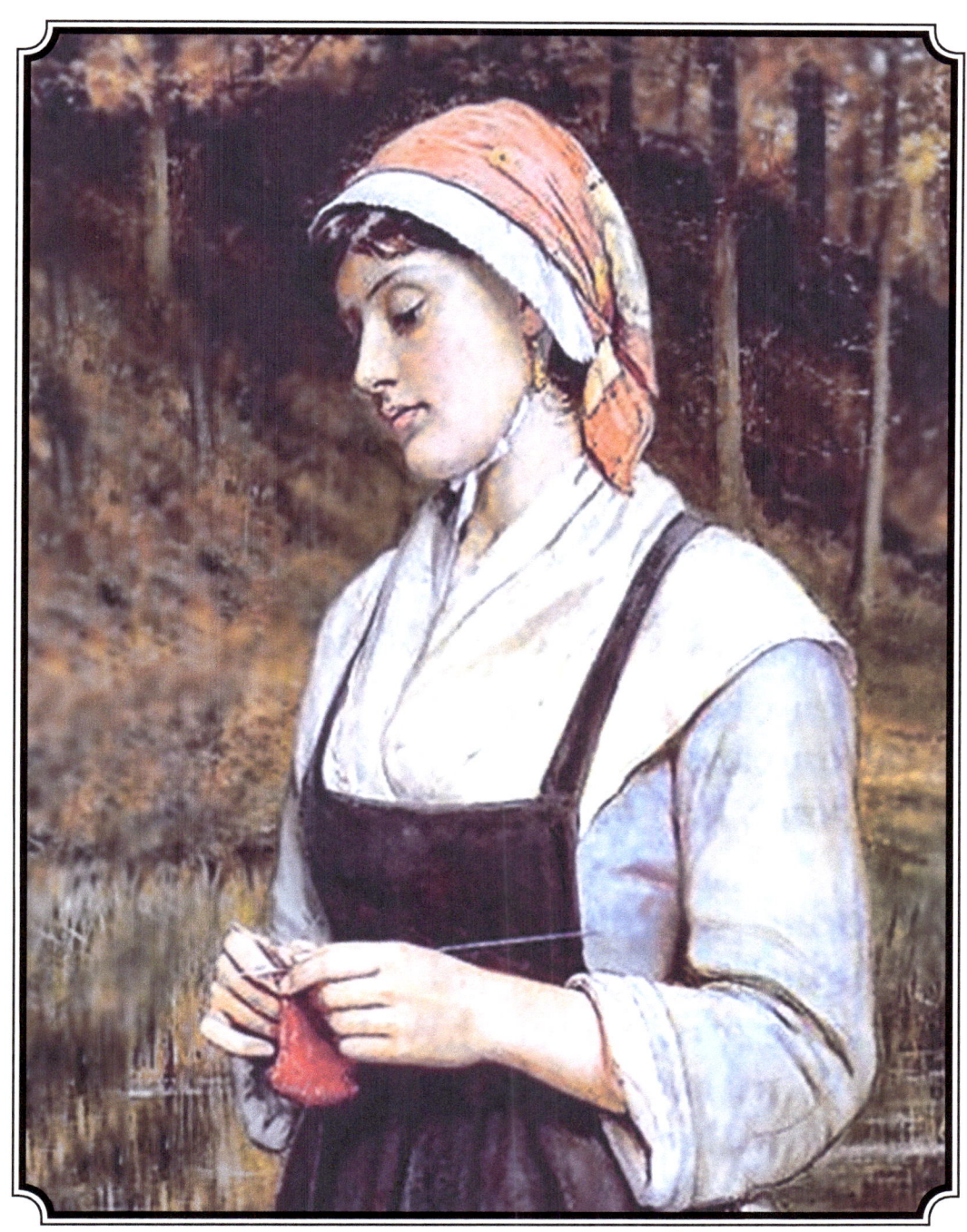

"Knitting", by Charles Sillem Lidderdale
Oil, 1888

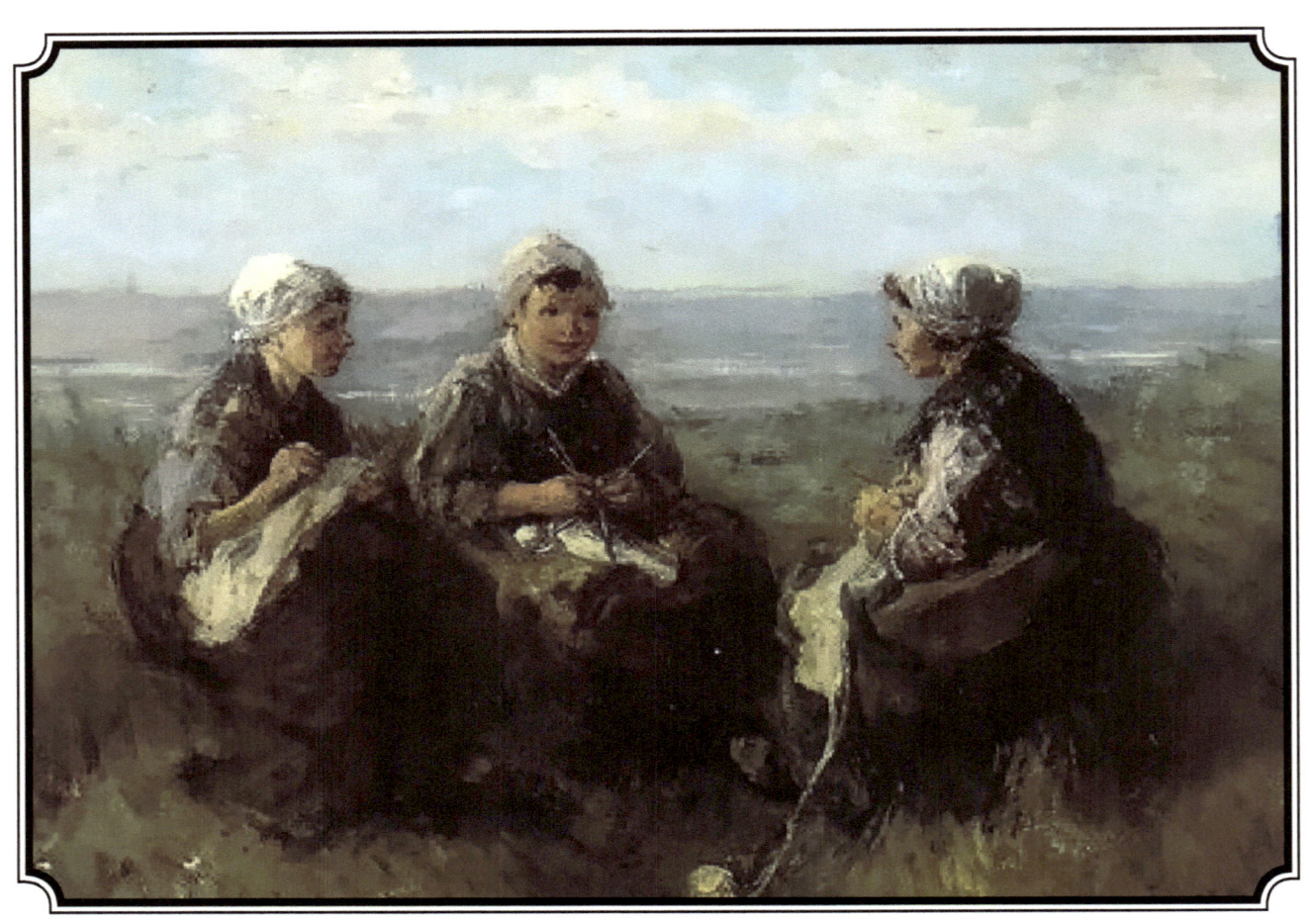

"Three Women Knitting by the Sea", by Jozef Israels
Oil, c.1860s

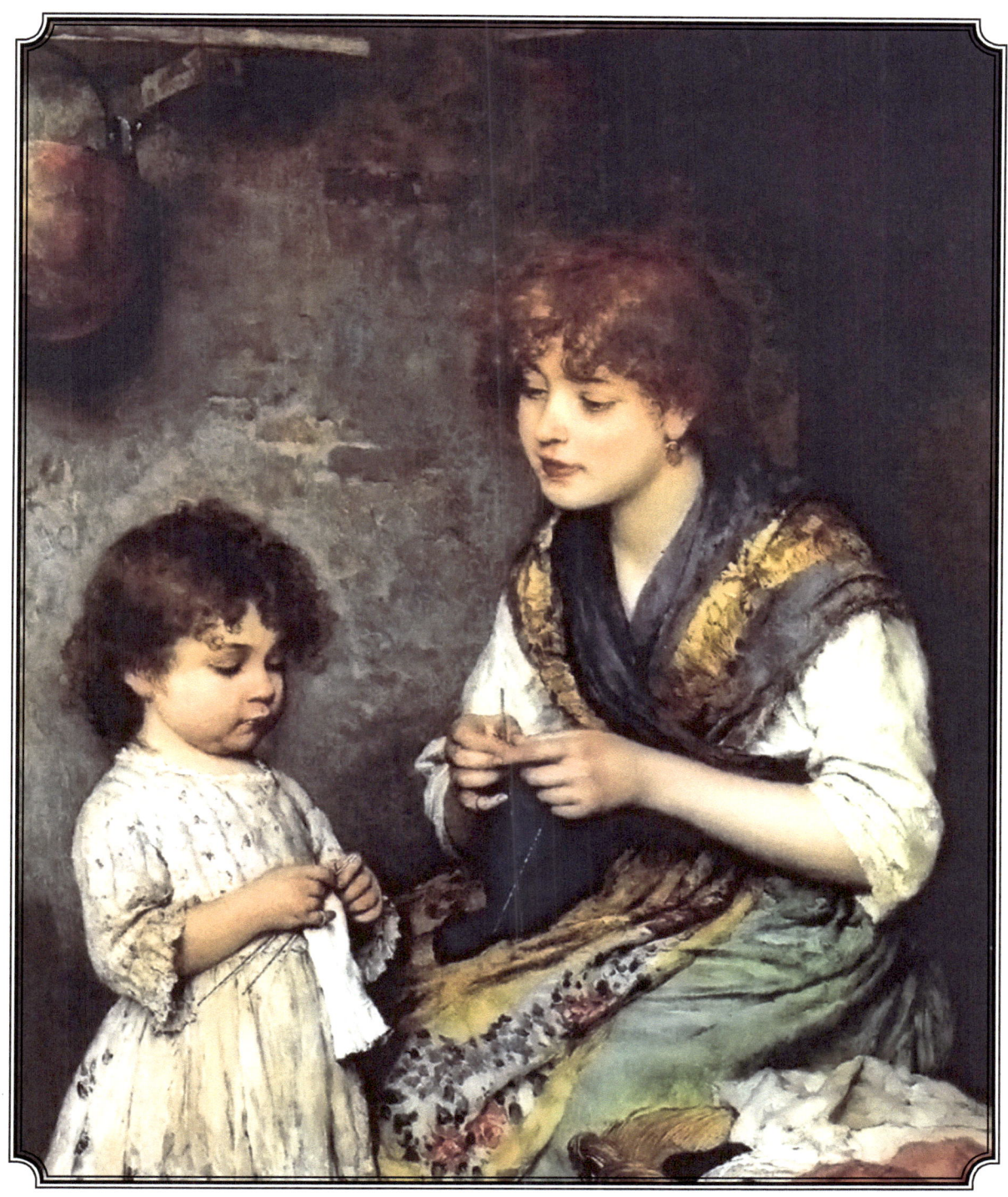

"The Knitting Lesson", by Eugene de Blaas
Oil, 1869

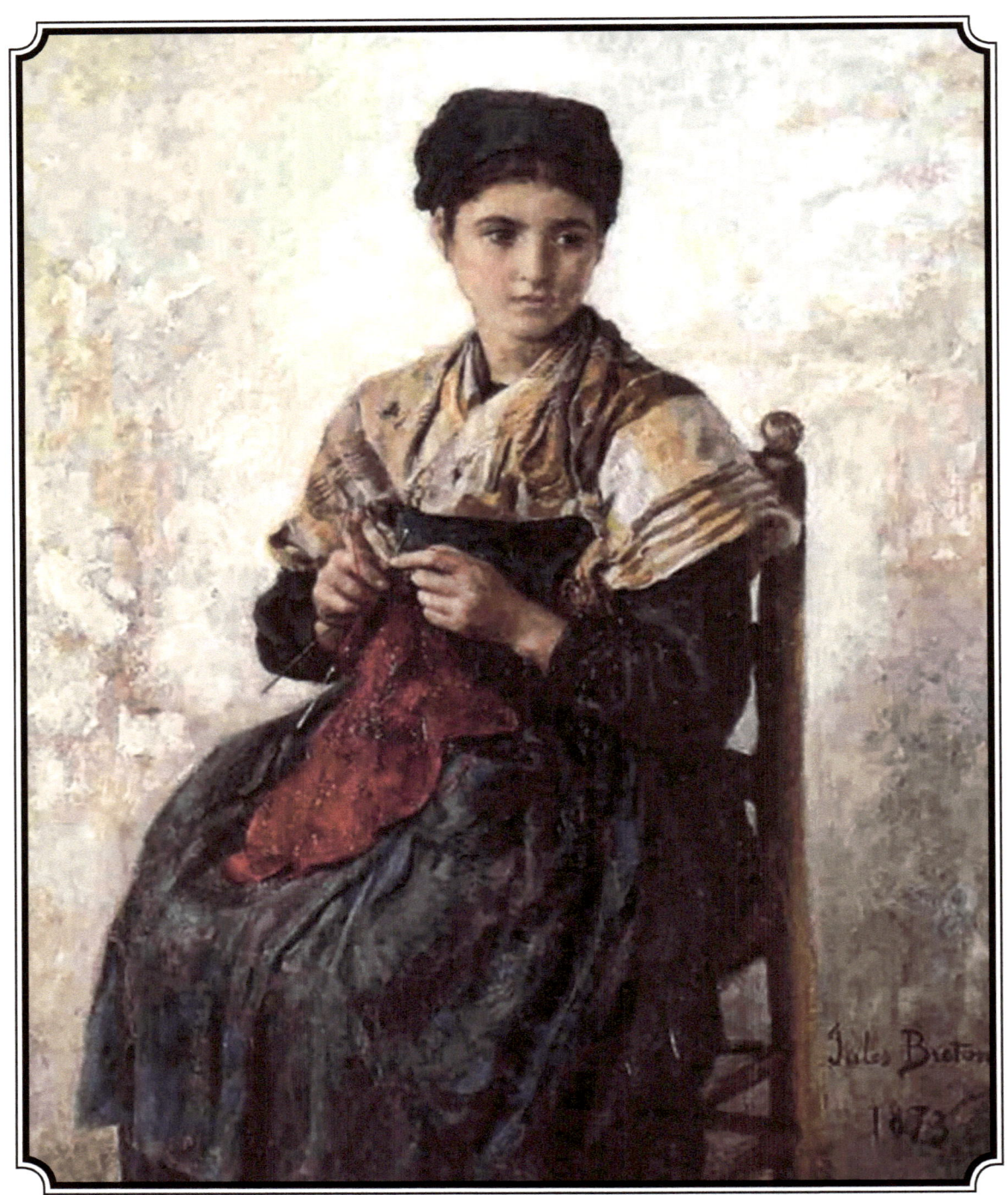

"Young Woman Knitting", by Jules Breton
Oil, 1873

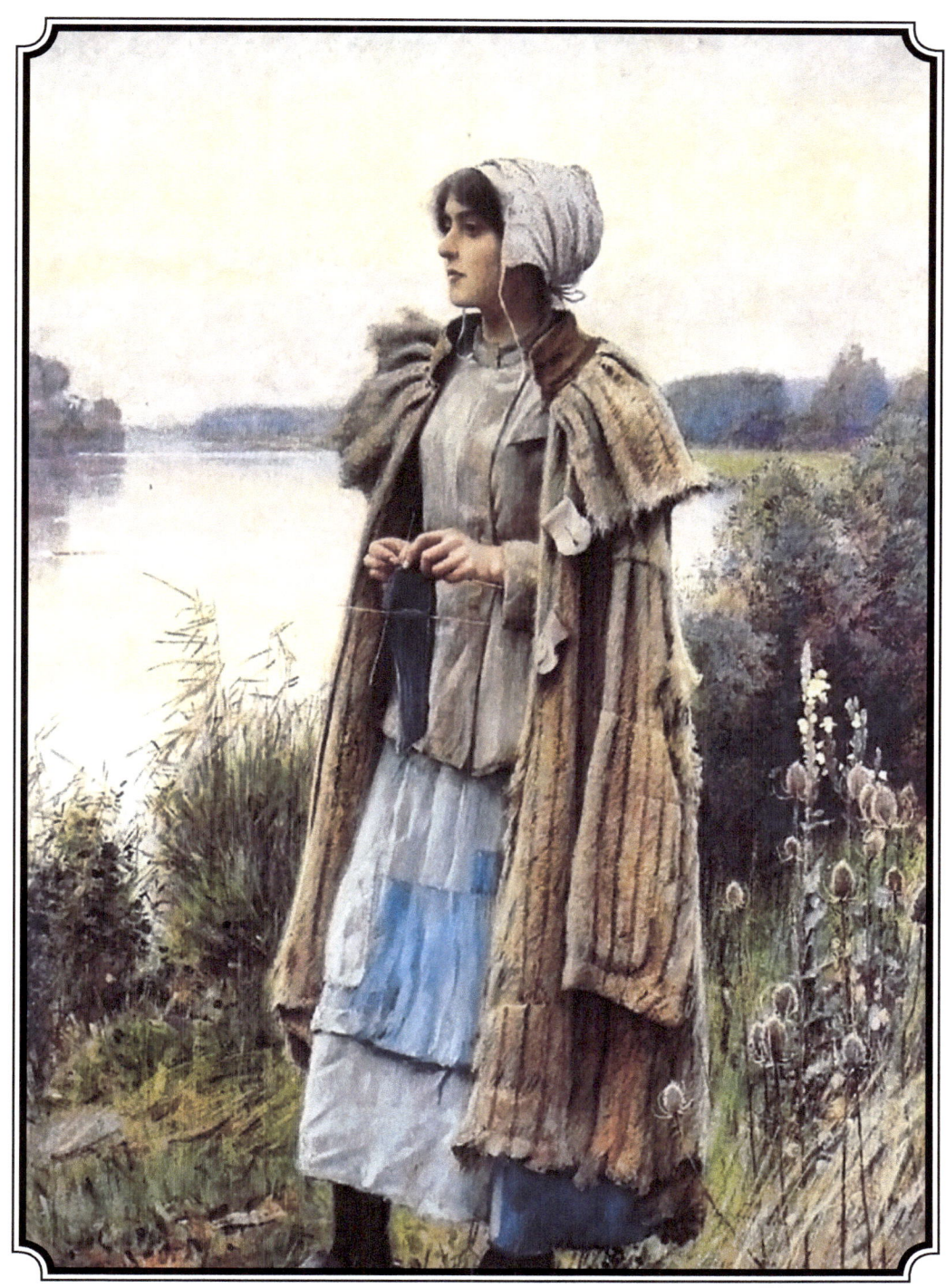

"Knitting in the Fields", by Charles Sprague Pearce
Oil, c.1860s

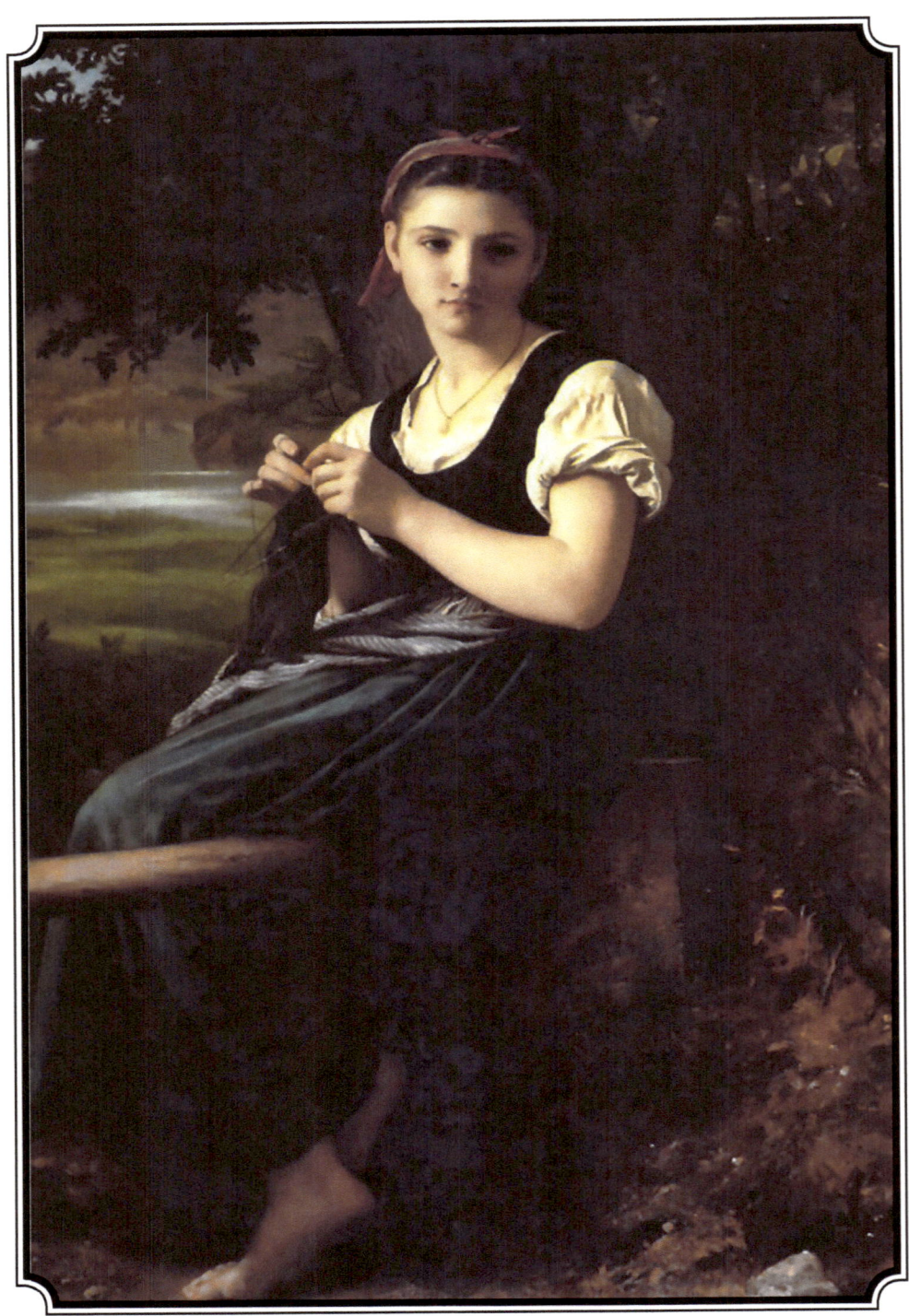

"The Tricoteuse", by William Adolphe Bouguereau
Oil, 1879

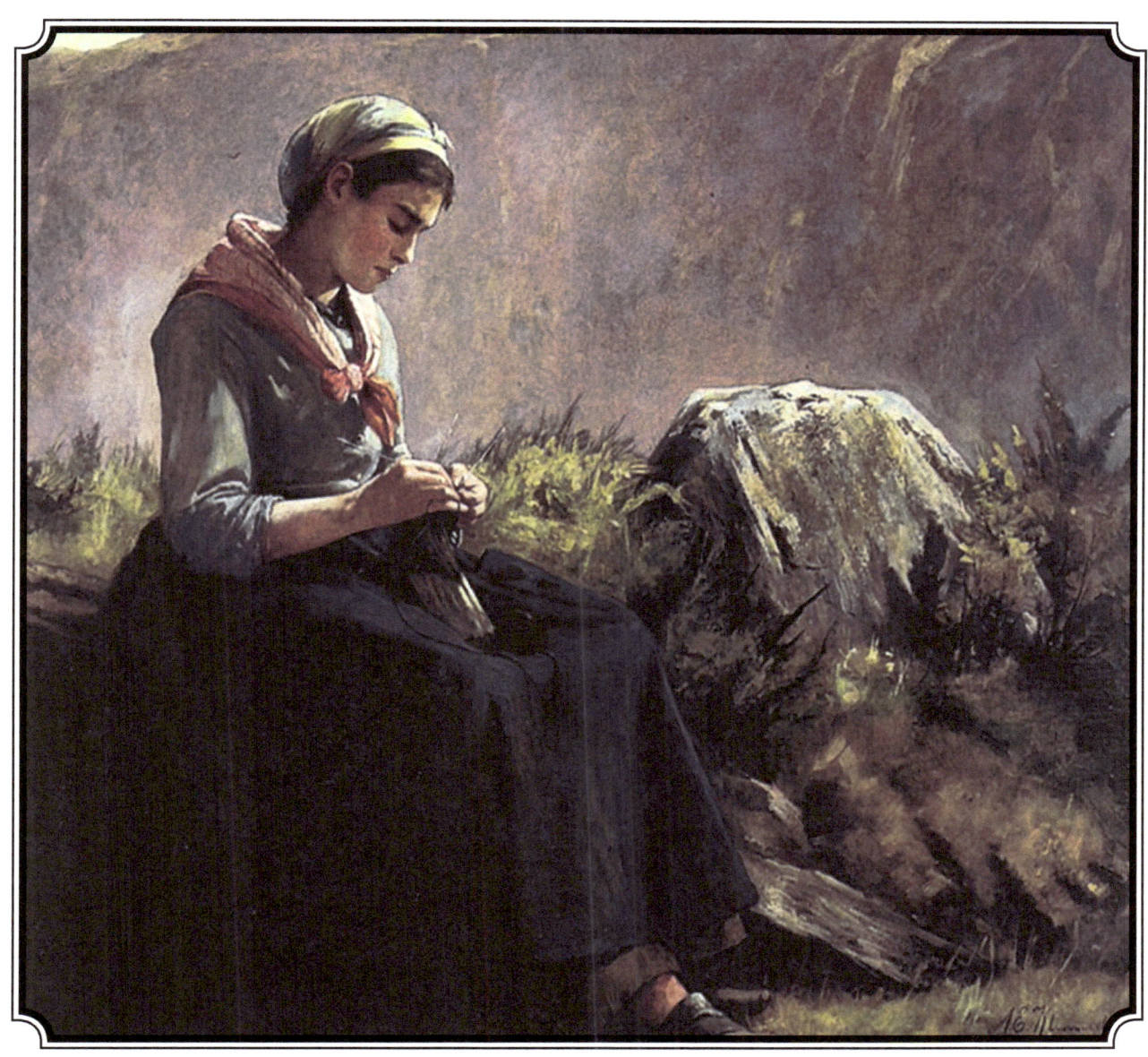

"Catinou Knitting", by Anna Elizabeth Klumpke
Oil, 1887

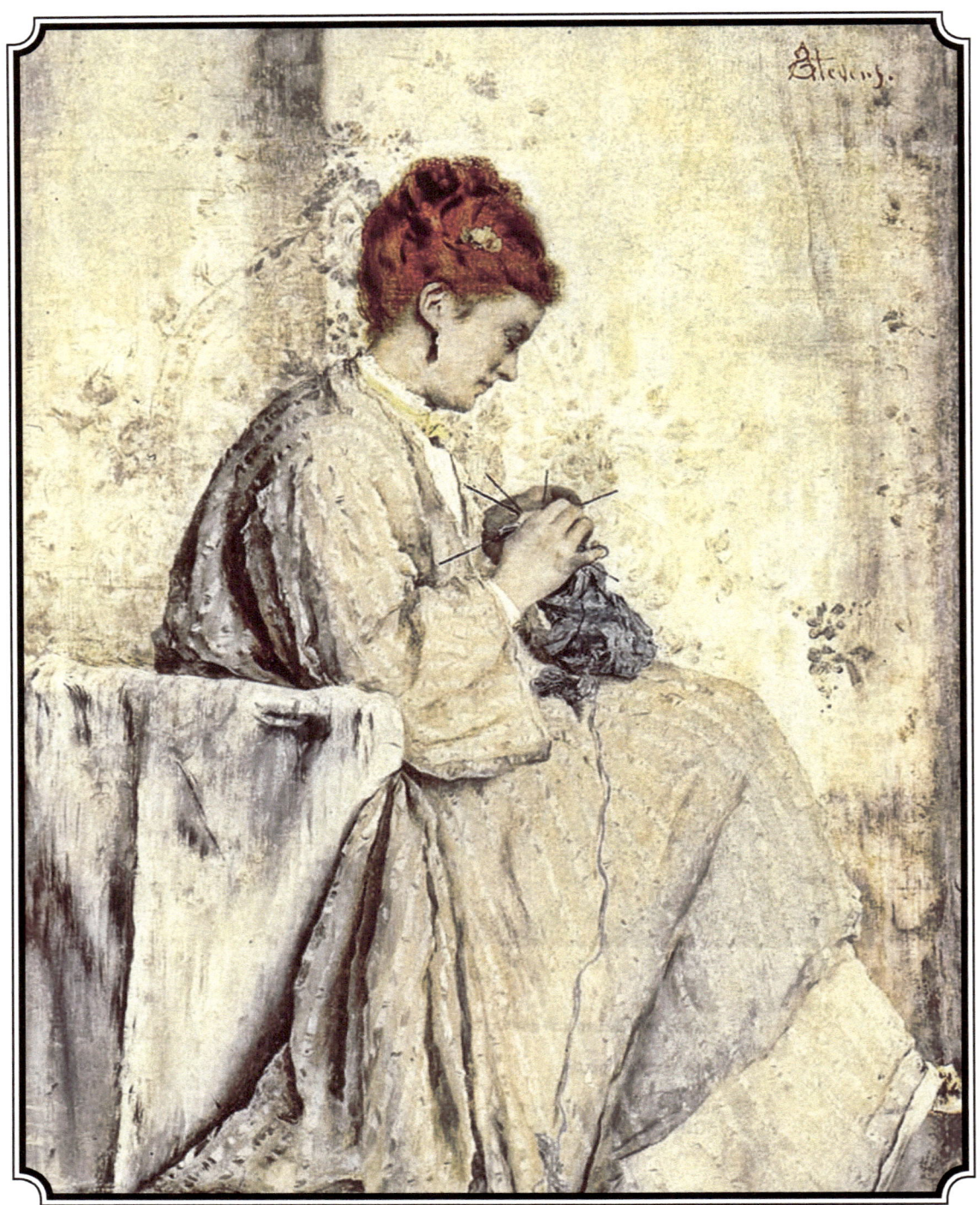

"The Knitter", by Alfred Stevens
Oil, c.1860s

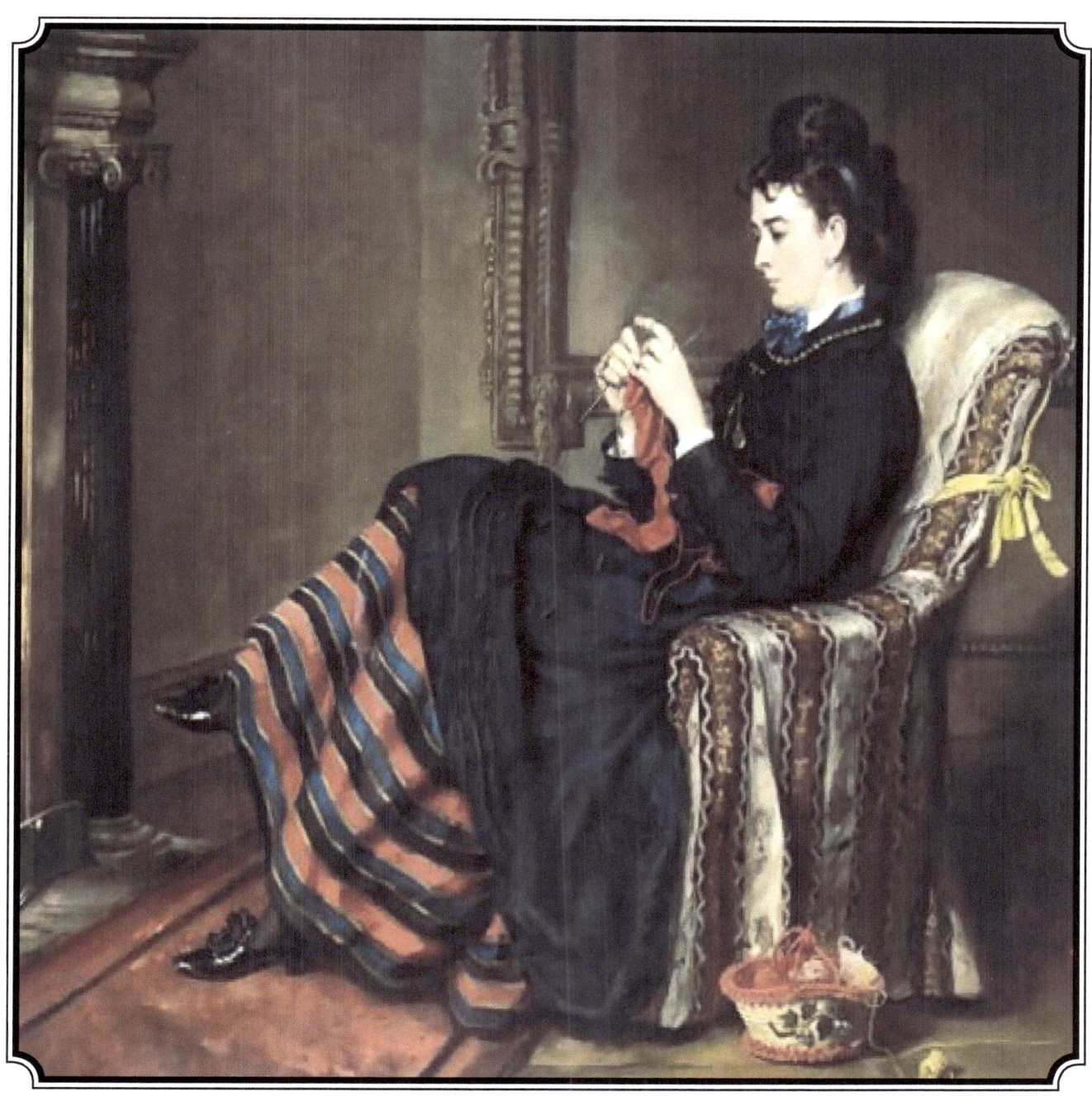

"Knitting A Stocking", by Sir Francis Grant
Oil, c.1860

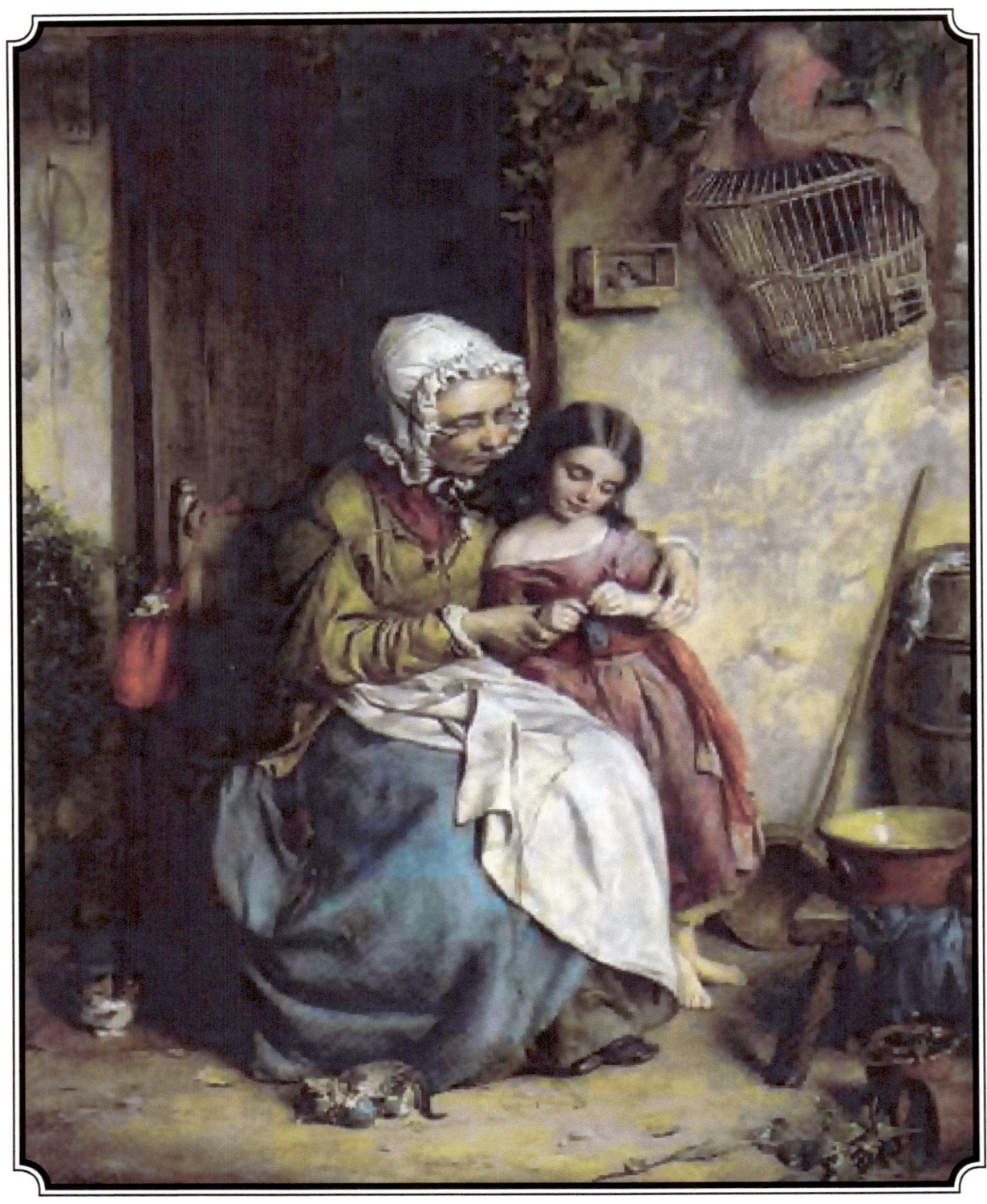

"Knitting Lesson", by John T. Peele
Oil, c.1858

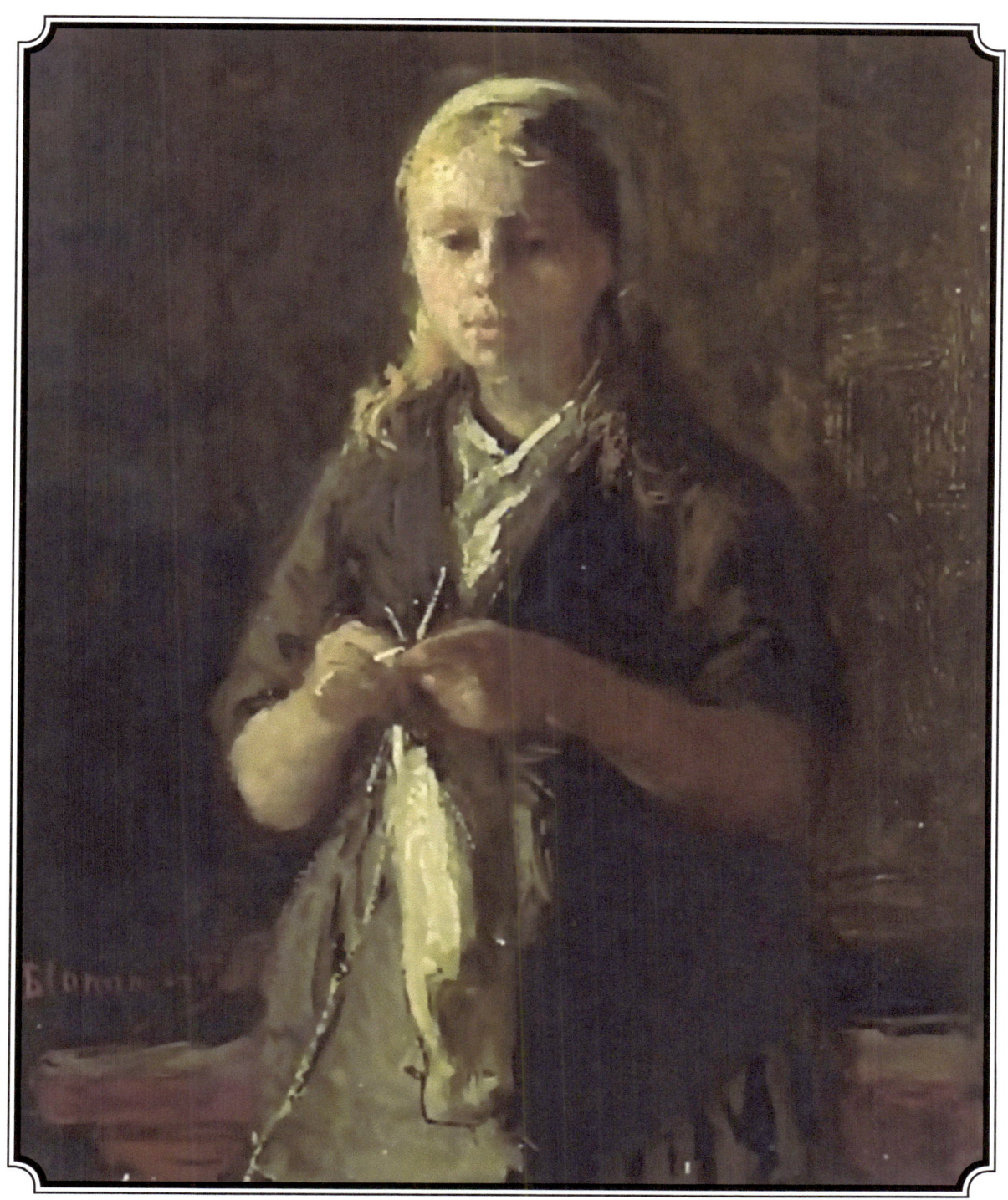

"Girl Knitting", by Bernardus Johannes Blommers
Oil, c.1800W

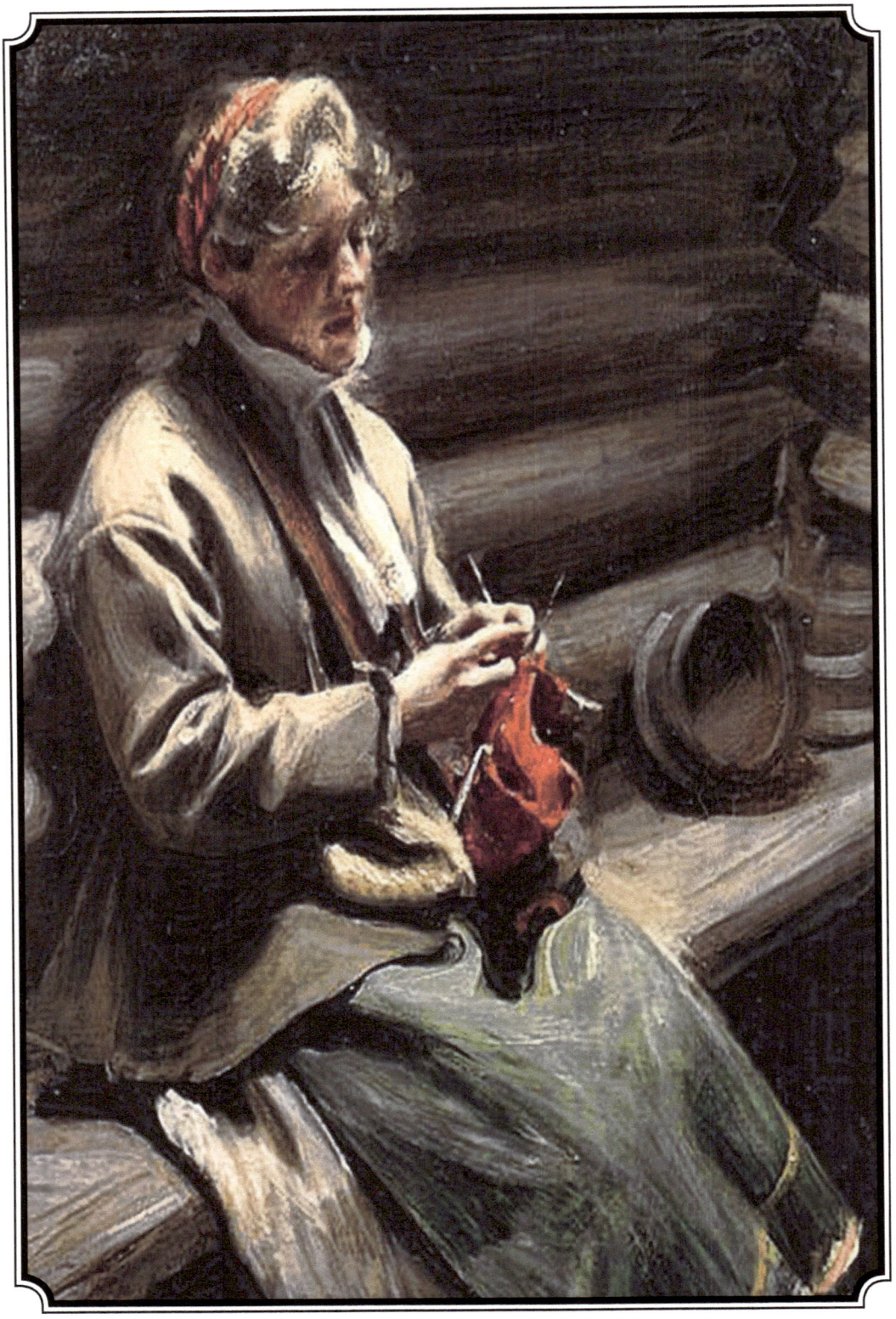

"Woman knitting", by Anders Zorn
Oil, c.1901

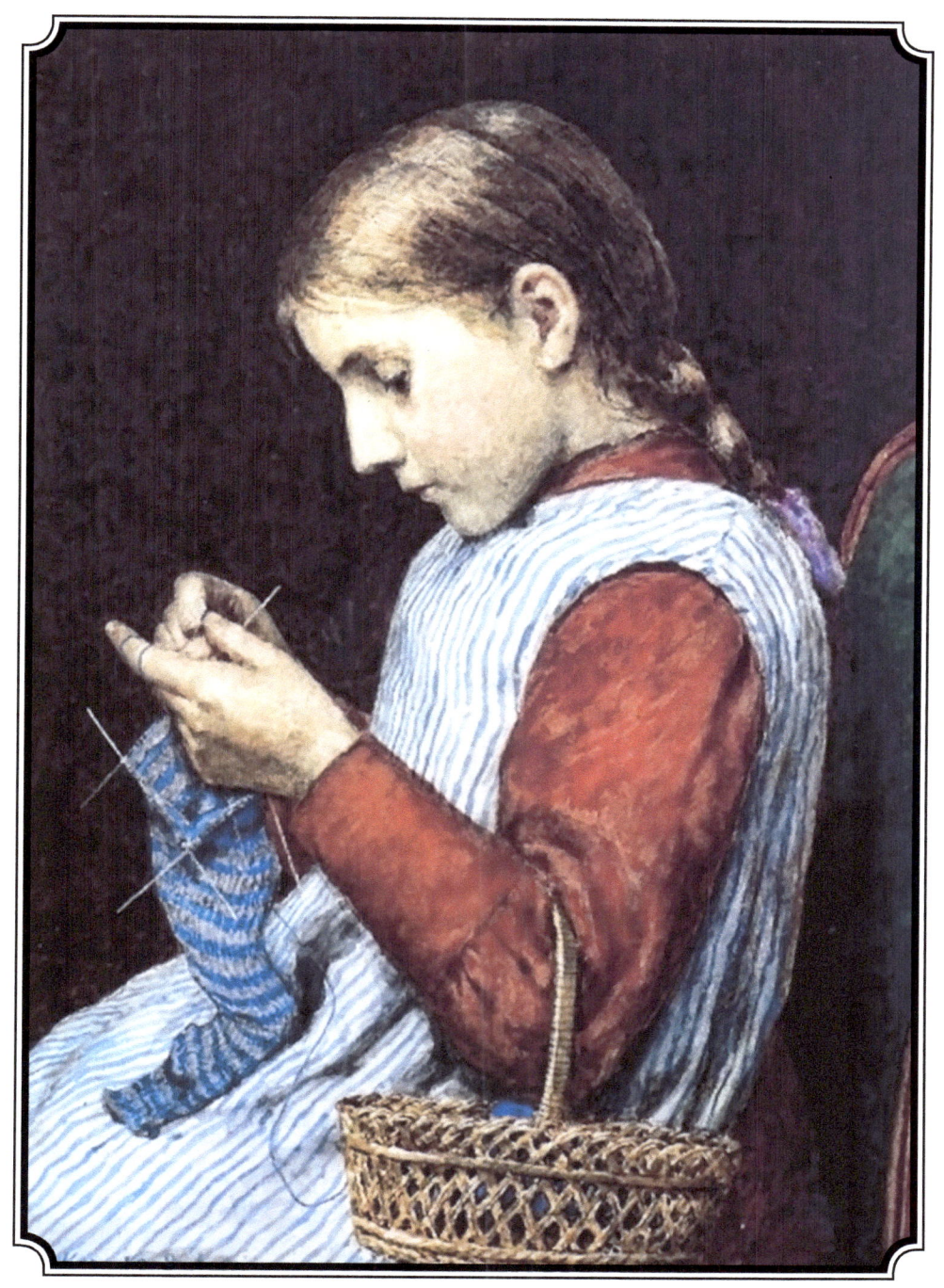

"Girl Knitting", by Alexei Alexeivich Harlamoff
Watercolor, c.1850s

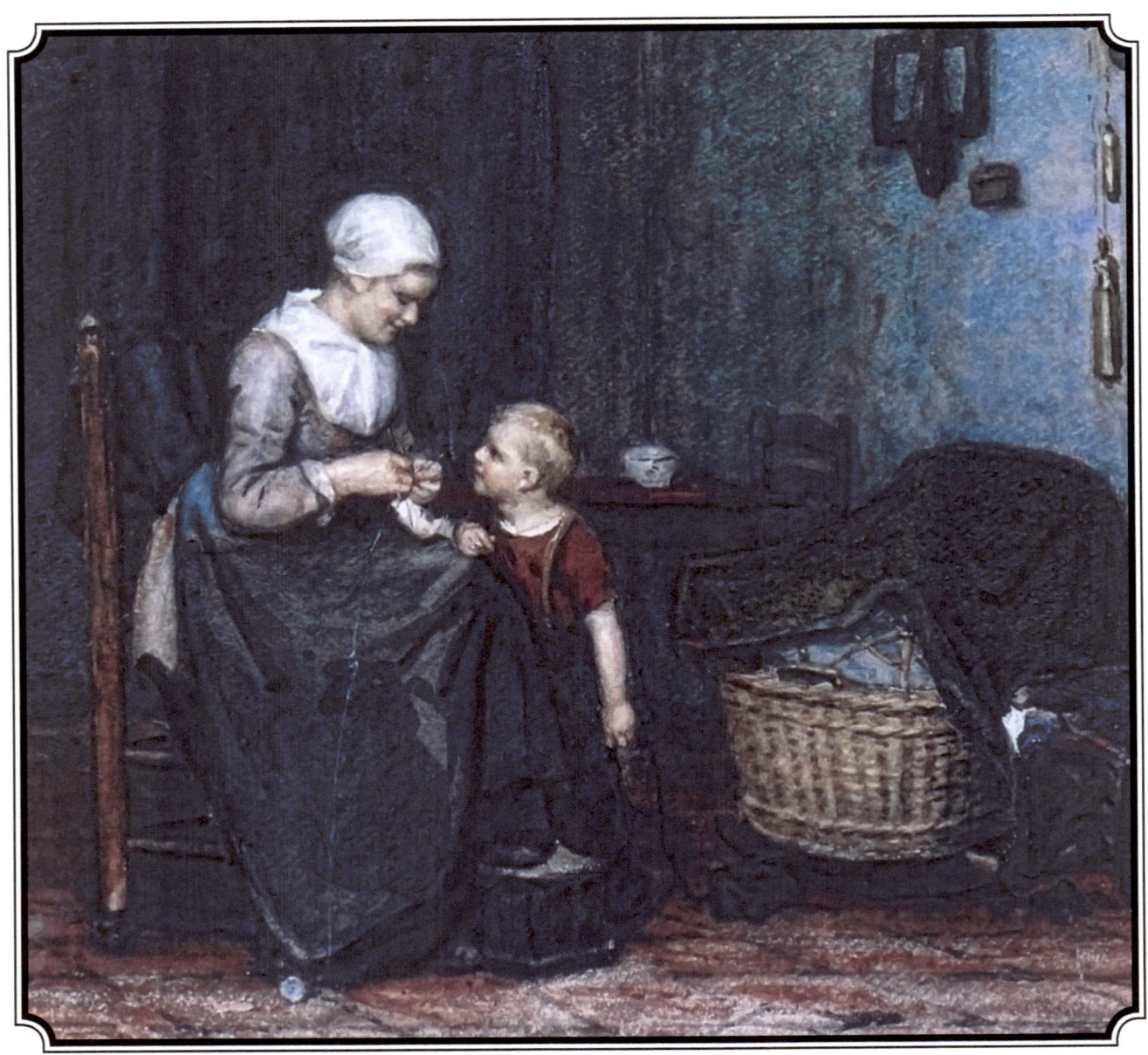

"Woman With Child Knitting", by Johannes Neuhuijs
Pastel, 1867

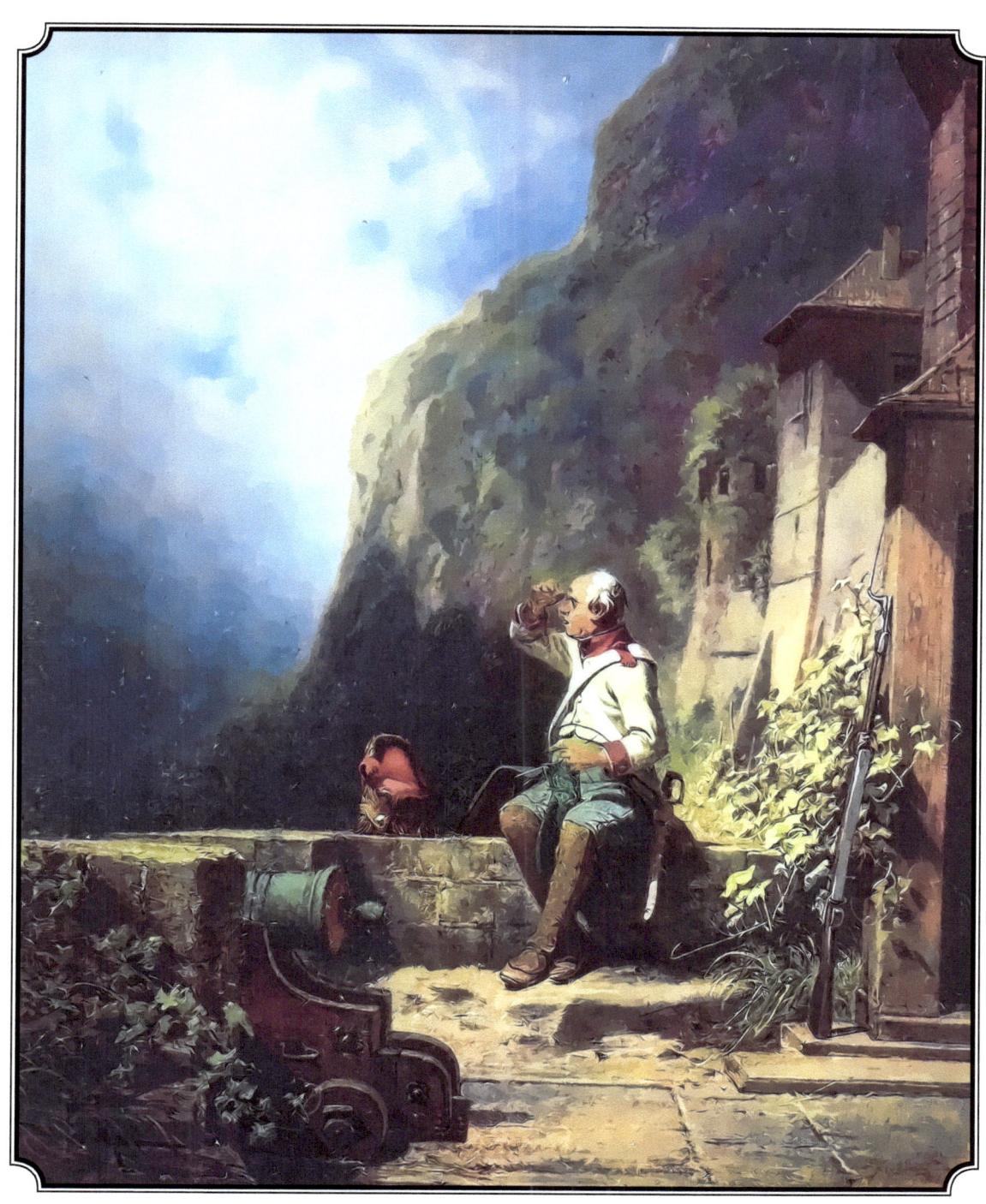

"The Knitting Look-Out", by Carl Spitzweg
Oil, 1850

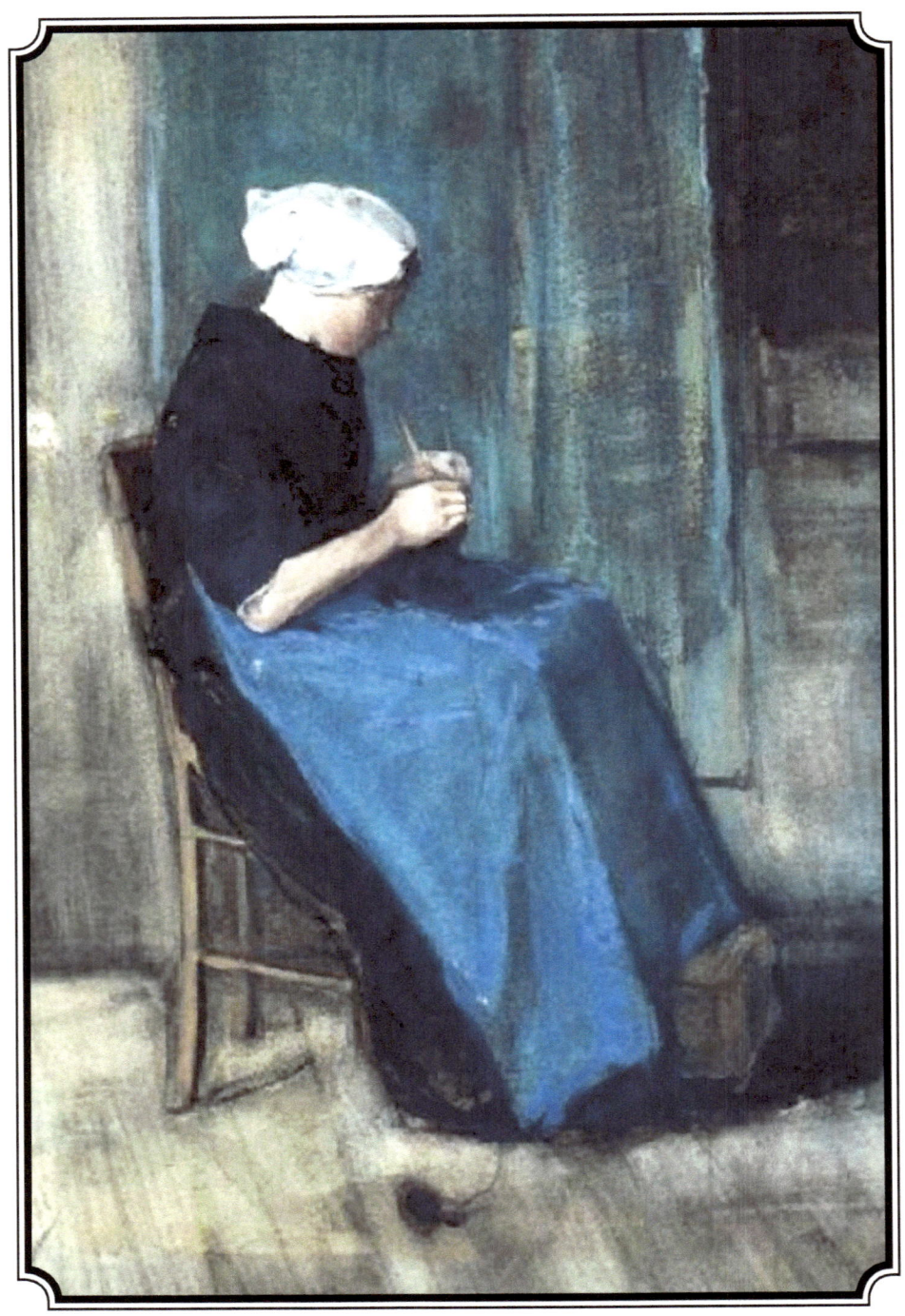

"Young Scheveningen Woman Knitting", by Vincent Van Gogh
Oil, 1888

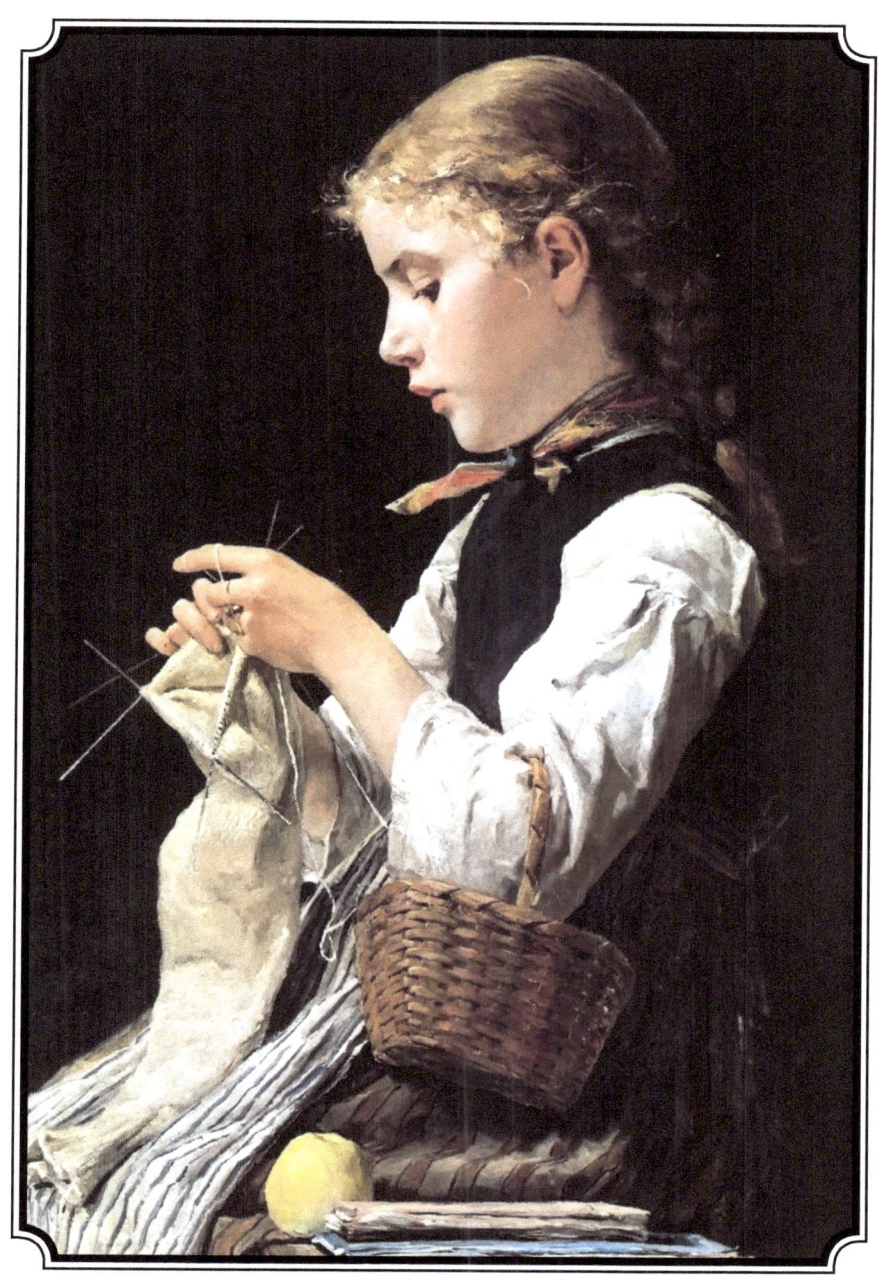

"Young Girl Knitting", by Carl Spitzweg
Oil, 1884

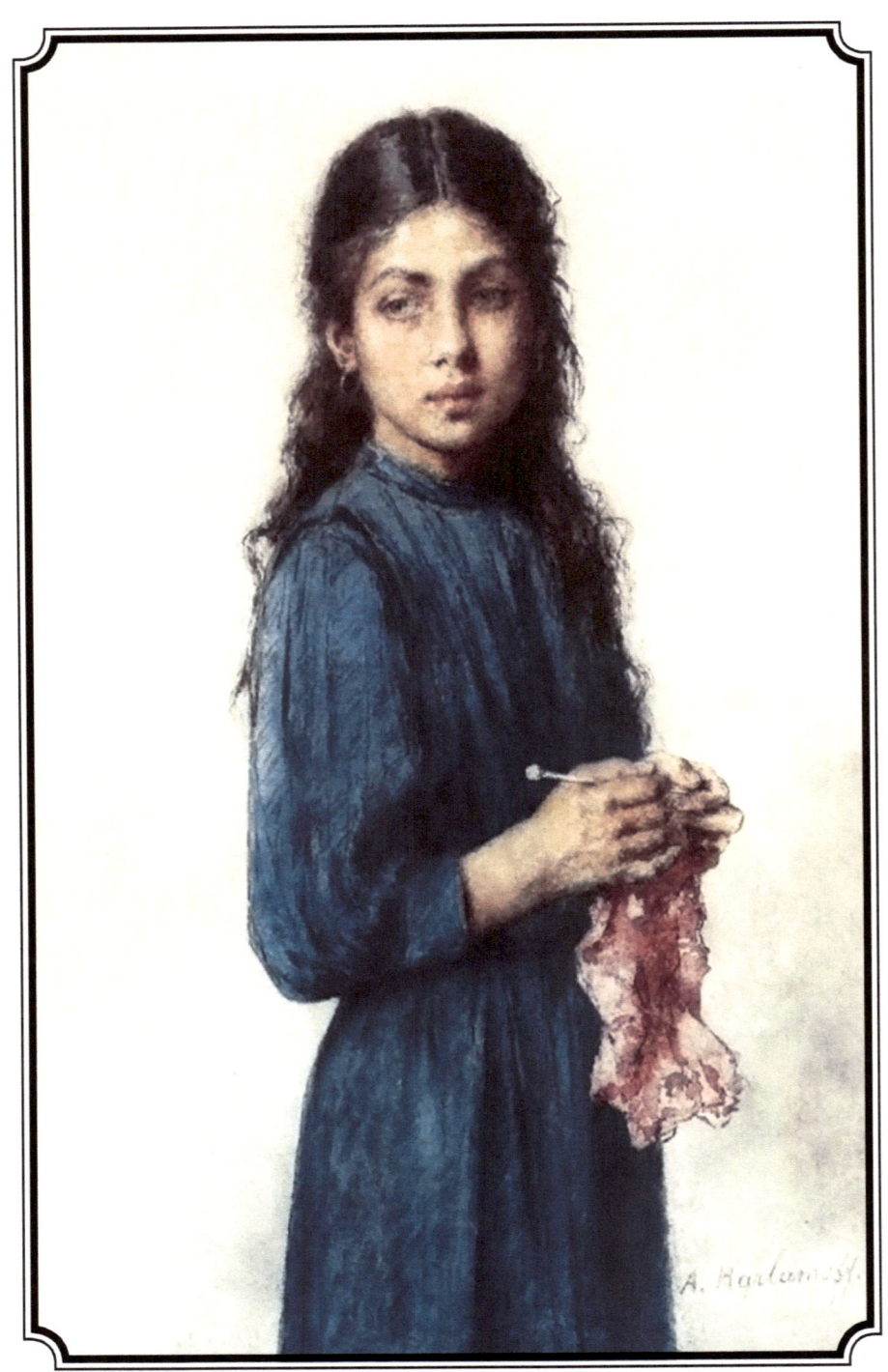

"Portrait of a Young Girl Knitting", by Alexei Harlamoff
Oil, 1845

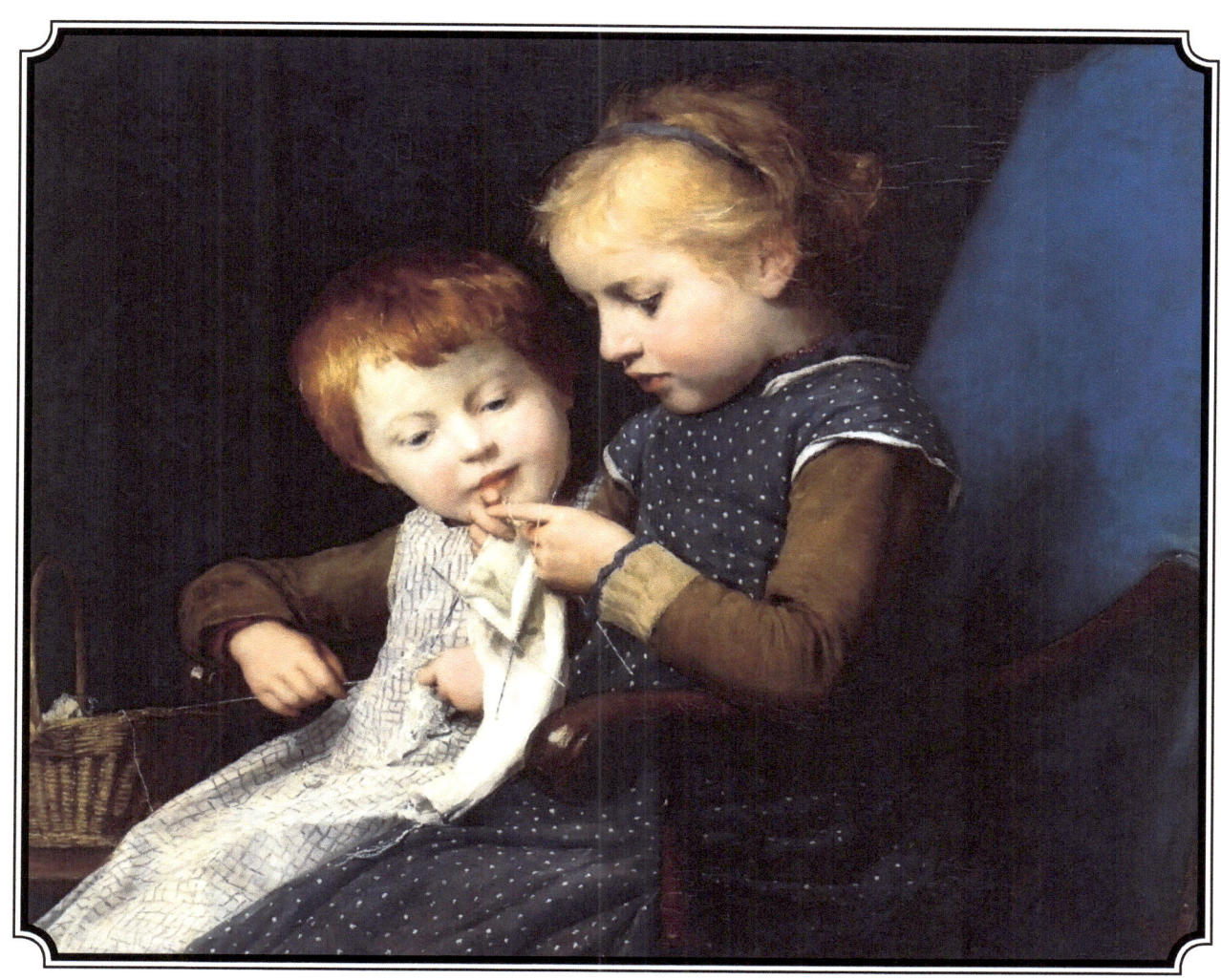

"Two Kids Knitting", by Albert Anker
Oil, c.1850s

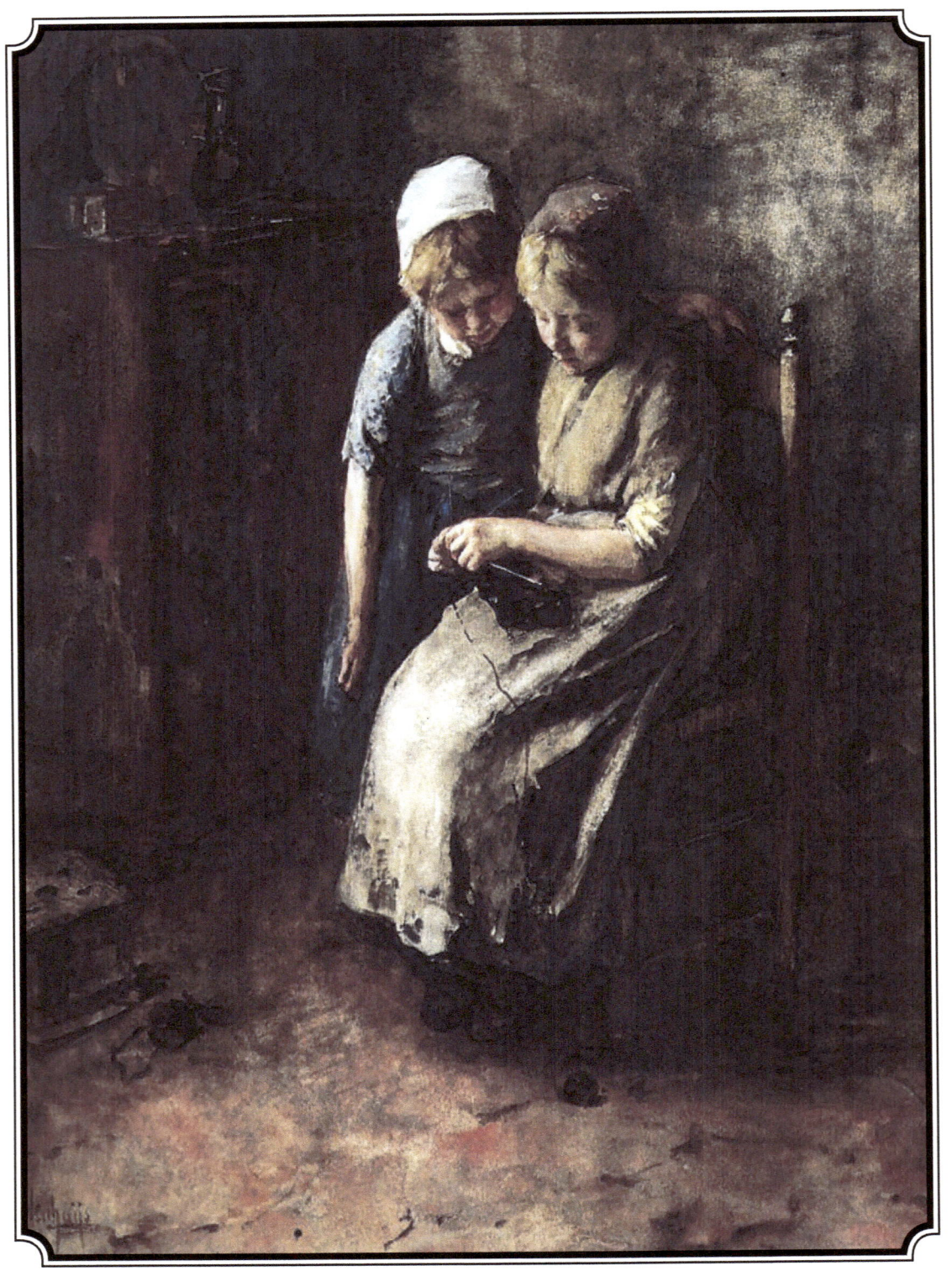

"Two Girls Knitting", by Johannes Albert Neuhuys
Oil, 1867

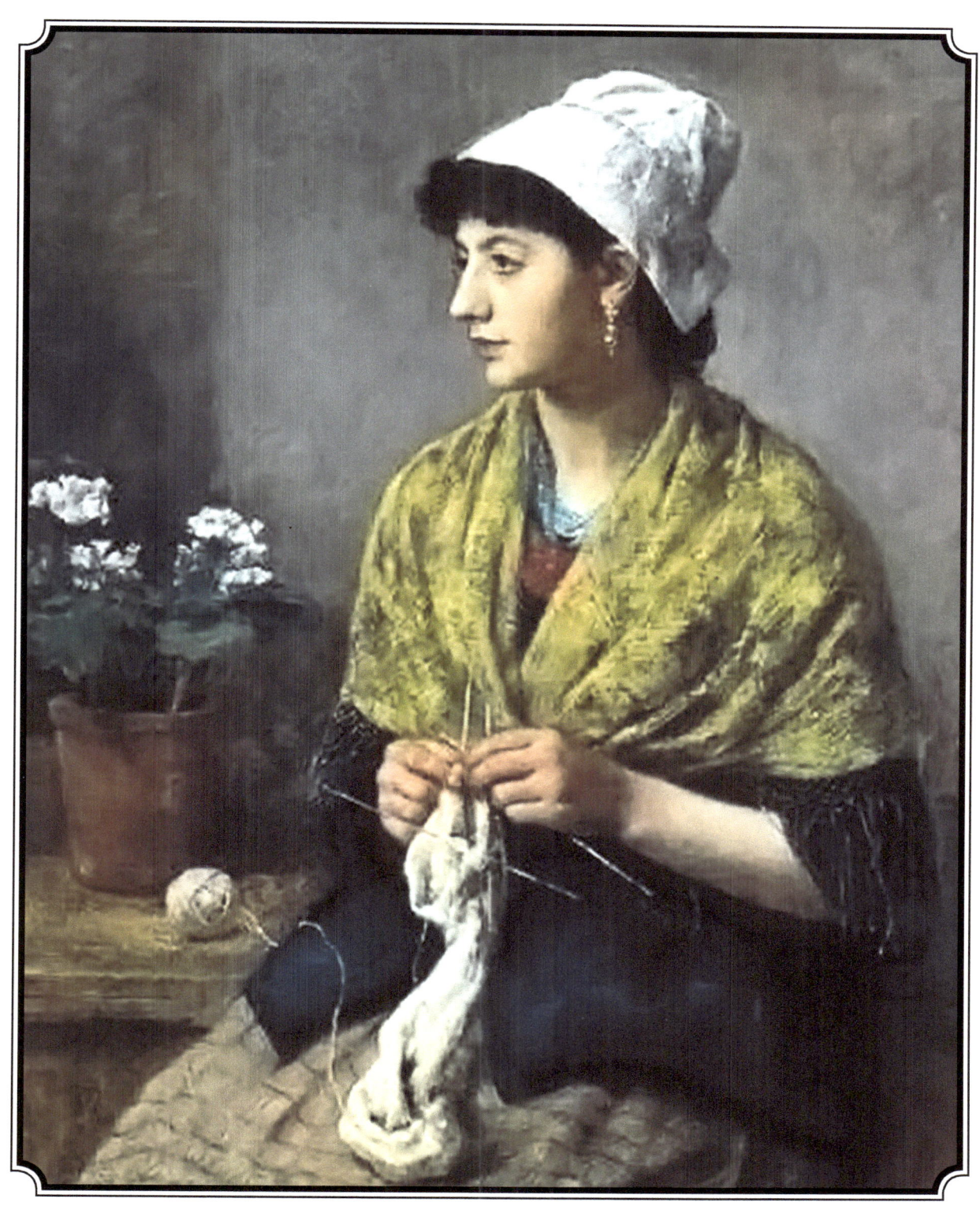

"Woman Knitting," by Otto Scholderer
Oil, 1860s

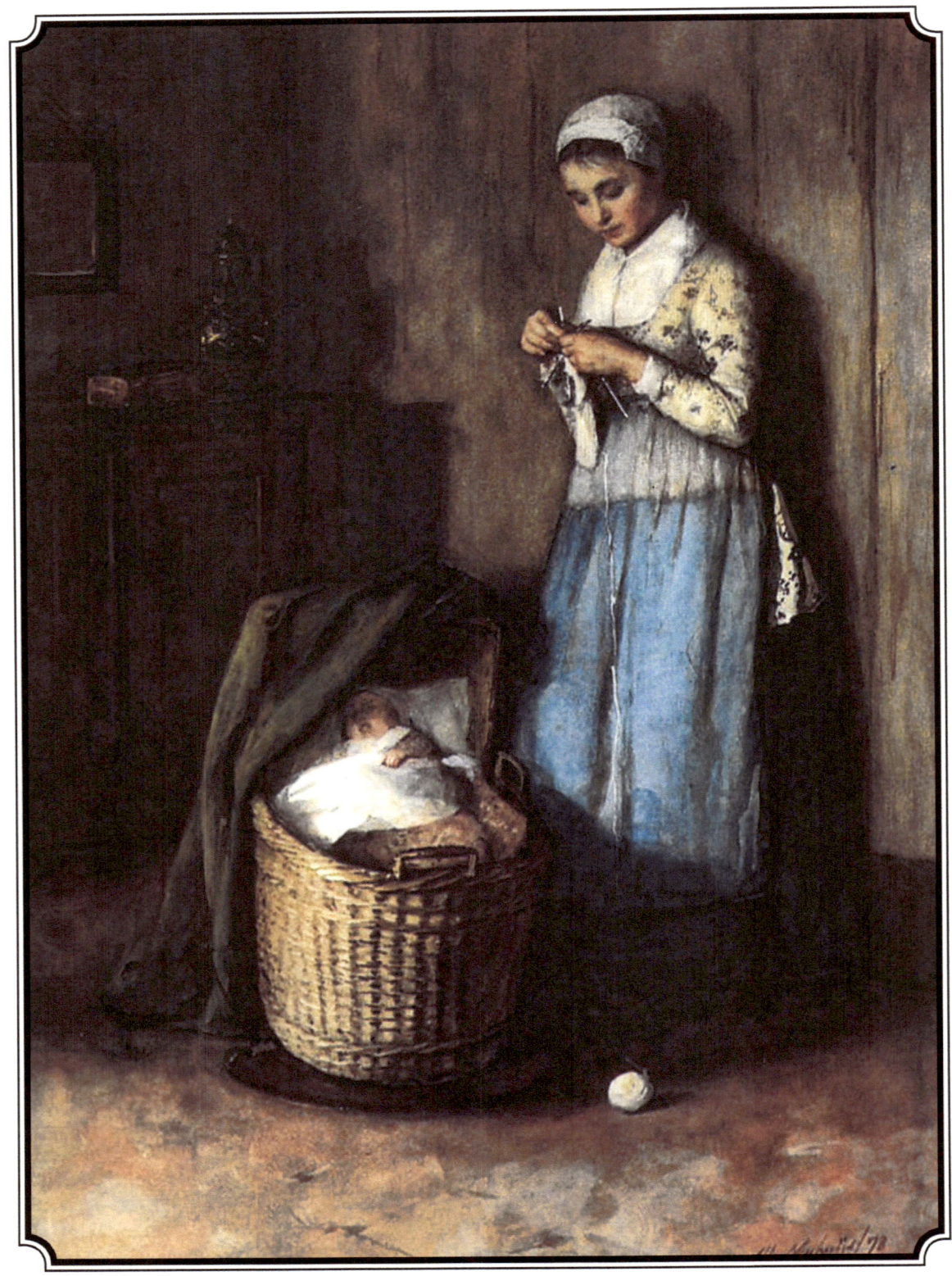

"Knitting Mother and Her Child", by Johannes Albert Neuhuys
Oil, 1878

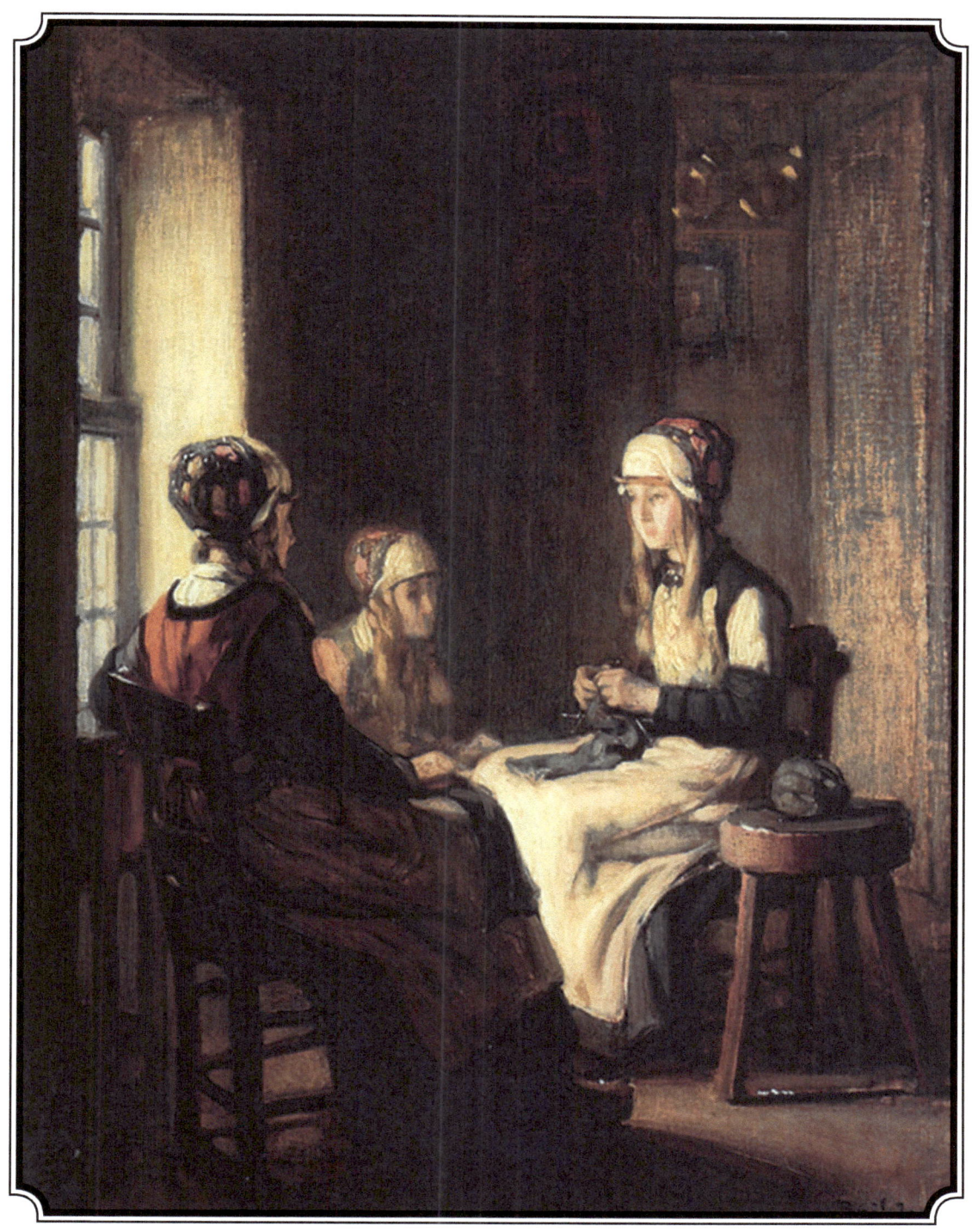

"An Interior With Marken Girls Knitting", by Claude Bail
Oil, 1872

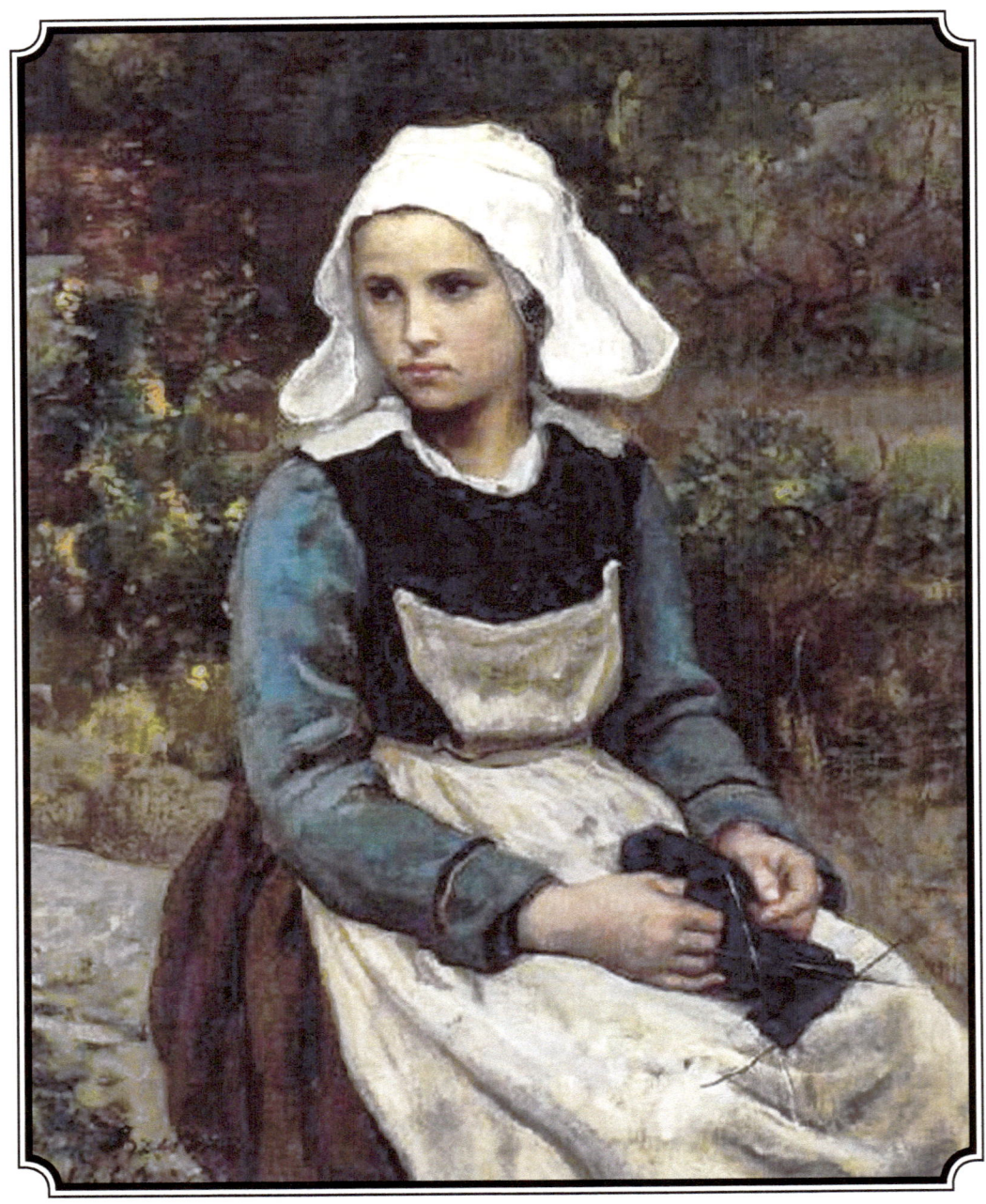

"Young Girl Knitting", by Jules Breton
Oil, 1874

Drawings & Prints

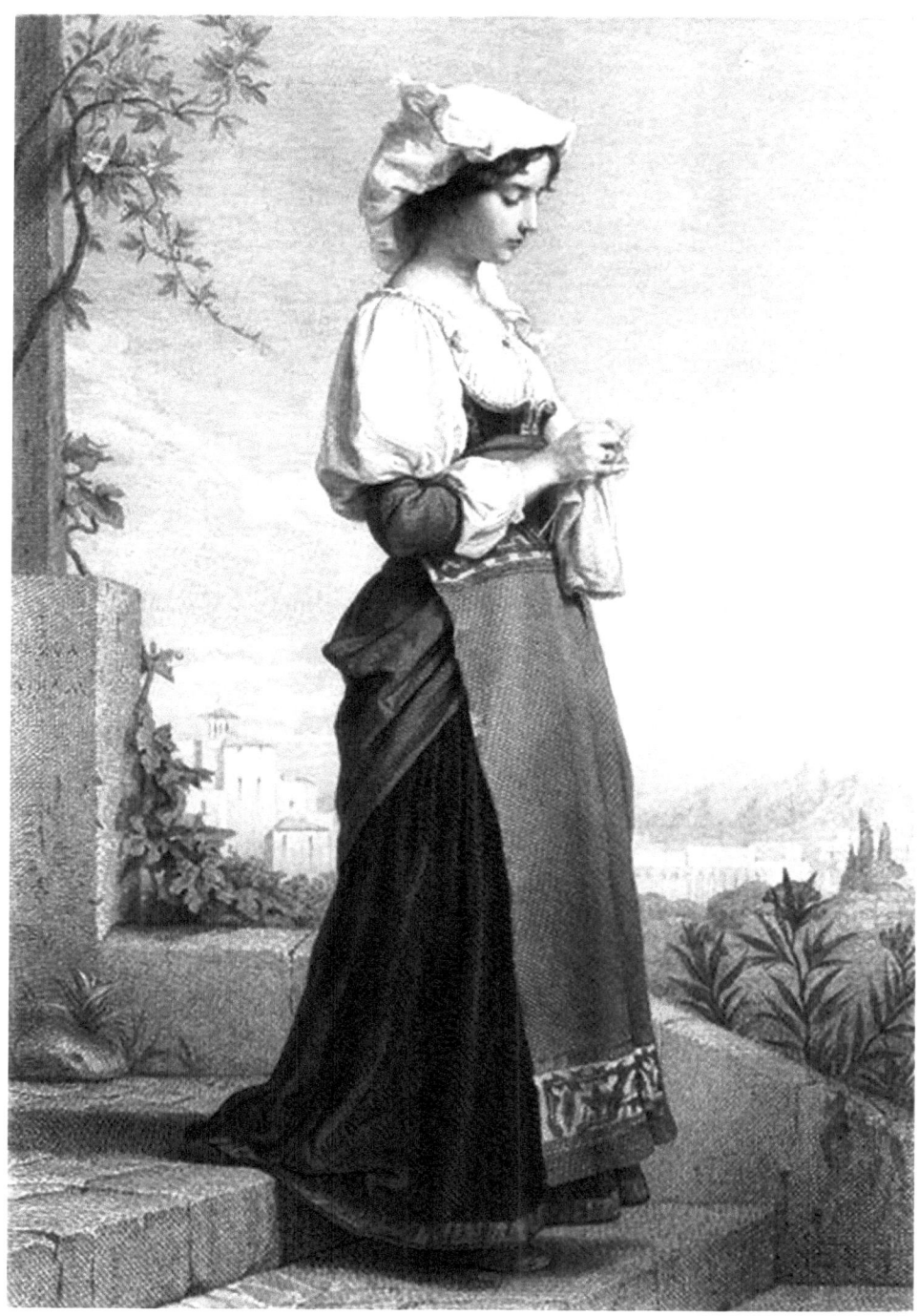

"Villanella", by Charles-François Levasseur
Print, c. 1800

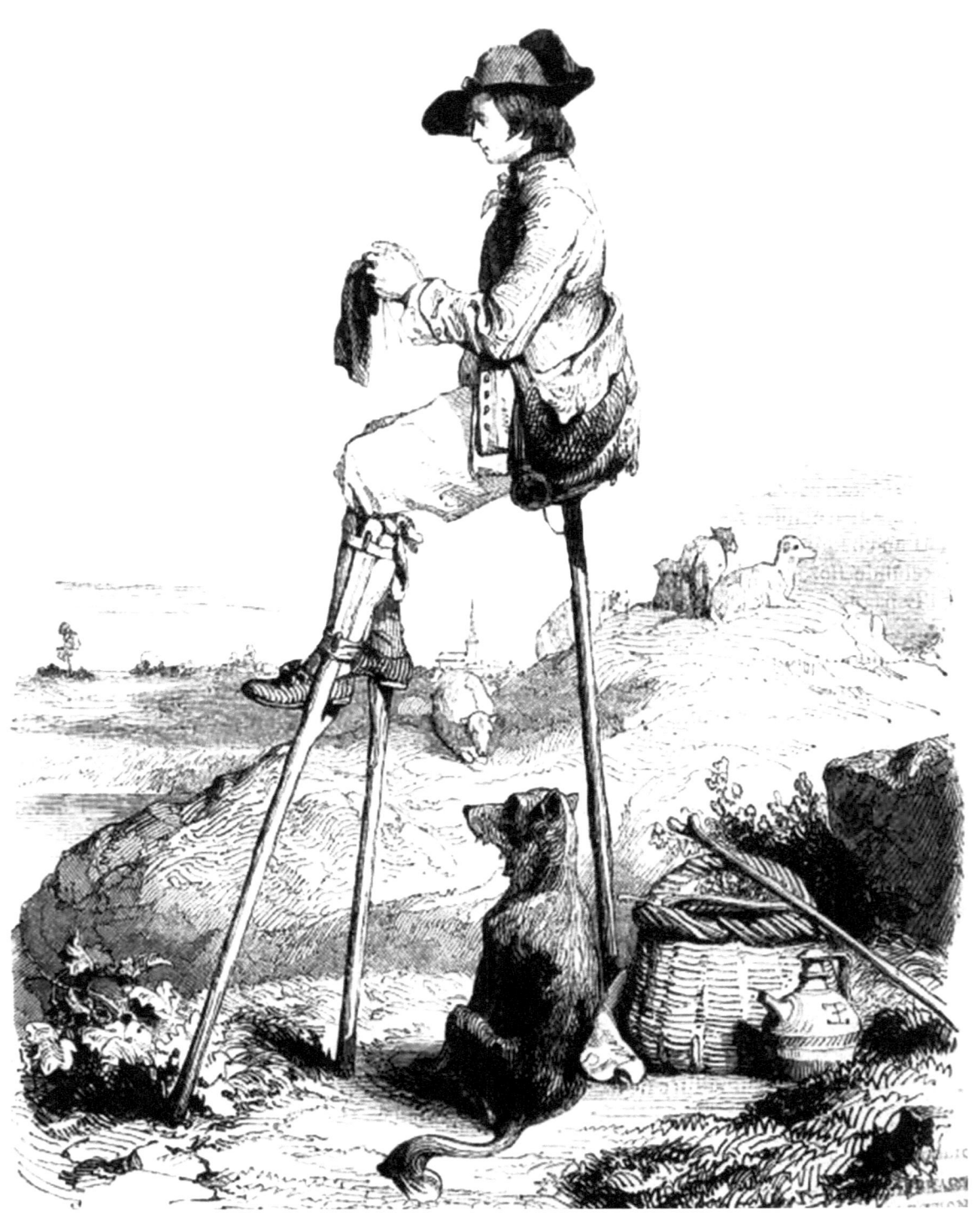

"Shepherd Resting and Knitting, by Francisco De Goya
Print, c.1800

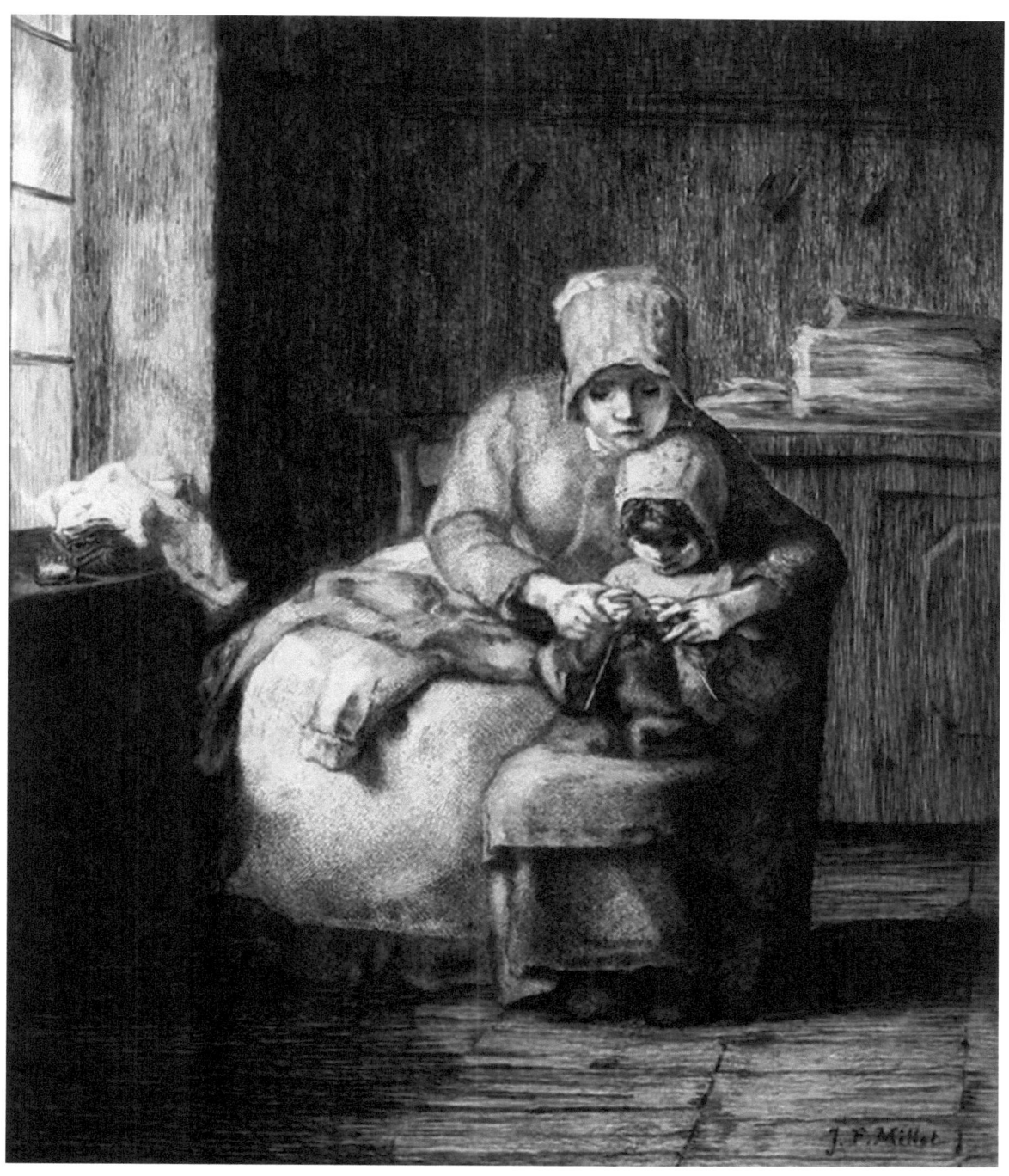

"The Knitting Lesson, by Jean-Francois Millet
Charcoal drawing, 1883

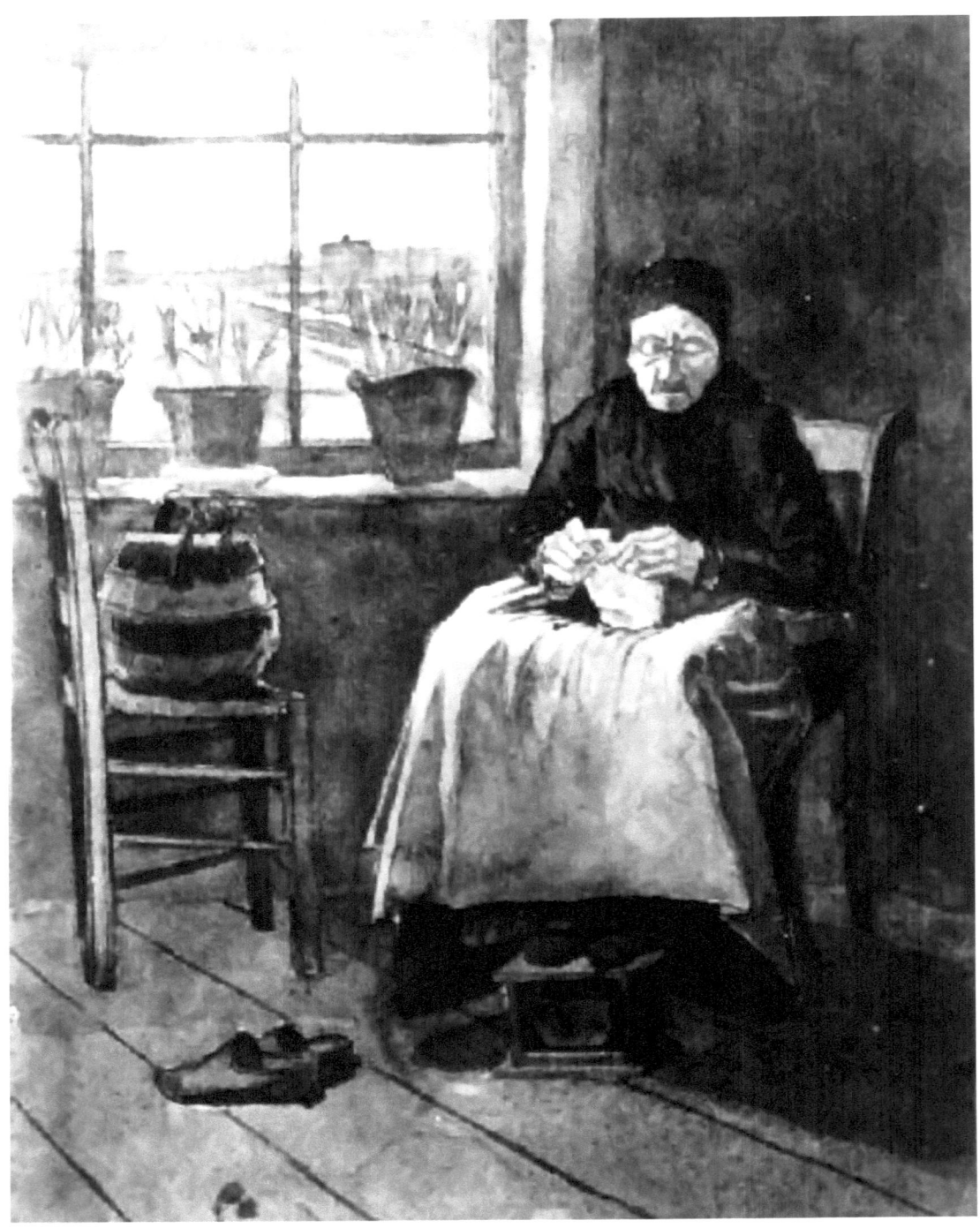

"Woman Carding Wool", by Jean-Francois Millet
Print, 1850

About the Author

Tulasi Zimmer is an award winning handspinner, professional artist, educator, and fiber artist. WW She art career expands into the fields of painting and drawing, graphic design, web design, multimedia production, and fiber arts. In 1999, Tulasi created the award winning website The Joy of Handspinning (JOH). JOH provides useful information, free video demonstrations, and publishes instructional materials that will enable anyone to learn how to handspin natural fibers into yarn with a drop spindle and/or spinning wheel. The JOH web site continues to be a popular resource on the topic of handspinning. Visit www.joyofhandspinning.com